Windowsill Science Centers

By Lynne Kepler

SCHOLASTIC
PROFESSIONAL BOOKS

NEW YORK • TORONTO • LONDON • AUCKLAND • SYDNEY

DEDICATION

To my very own window watchers, Jake, Ty, and Muir.

.

ACKNOWLEDGMENTS

Special thanks to Kim Mays and her third graders at
Clarion-Limestone Elementary School in Strattanville, Pennsylvania,
for their enthusiasm and cooperation
in testing many of the activities in this book.

Edited by Joan Novelli
Cover design by Vincent Ceci and Jaime Lucero
Cover illustration by Karen Fitz-Maurice
Interior design by Solutions by Design, Inc.
Interior illustrations by James Graham Hale

ISBN#0-590-74395-3
Copyright ©1996 by Lynne Kepler

Contents

yeast-bread
Tea
sprouts

About this Book

I've always spent a lot of time looking out windows—wondering about, learning from, and admiring the world just on the other side of the glass. All three of my children have been looking out windows, too, since they were only a few months old. Before they could talk, my husband and I would point to falling snowflakes or birds sitting at feeders. Once the kids began to talk, they started making their own observations and always had plenty of questions! "Why do birds come to our bird feeder?" "How come all the leaves don't fall?" "How do the clouds move?" The most frequently asked one—"What's the weather going to be like today?"—usually came in the same breath as "Can I wear shorts today?" Windows are without a doubt an invitation for learning about what happens in the world and how it directly affects our lives.

What can your students see outside their classroom window? Do they notice the weather? The colors of leaves? Birds flying about? A classroom windowsill science center is a wonderful way to involve children in what they are naturally trying to do—understand their world. With the activities in this book, children will work with their classmates, talking and listening, writing and drawing, measuring and comparing. And while all of this is going on, they'll develop a connectedness with their own backyards—the kind of relationship that provides a solid foundation for reaching out and understanding the larger world.

—Lynne Kepler

SETTING UP FOR WINDOWSILL SCIENCE

As you think about setting up your windowsill science center, you will probably be asking yourself a few questions.

- How much space do I need?
- Does it matter which way my windows face?
- What kinds of materials will I need?

A 10-foot windowsill area will provide you with plenty of space. Your windows can face any direction; just be aware of how this may affect various activities. For activities that require direct sunlight, you may need to make a few adjustments. For example, if you are growing plants on your windowsill (see Sowing Seeds, page 58), you will want to choose plants that match the light conditions in your classroom.

If your classroom is without any windowsills, think about adopting one. Maybe you can borrow a section of windowsill in the school library or the main office. Or think about teaming up with a colleague whose classroom has win-

Decorate your windowsill science center with customized curtains made from old, light-colored sheets. Let children decorate the sheets with fabric crayon or paint. Hang from either side of the center, add a colorful cardboard valance, and your windowsill center will feel like home!

dows. Speaking of teaming up, consider having windowsill pen pals. Your students can compare results of their windowsill-based investigations with those of another class down the hall, on the other side of town, or even the other side of the country!

HOW TO USE THIS BOOK

Each of the eight windowsill science centers follows the same format, making it easy for you to plan and allow more time to focus on students. From process skills to assessment and extension ideas, here's what you'll find.

1. PROCESS SKILLS

The process skills that students will use to explore the concepts developed at each center are listed at the beginning of the center plans. This information can help you select areas of focus as you guide students in their work.

2. HANDS-ON ACTIVITIES

Each center features several hands-on activities. In most cases, materials are simple, inexpensive, and easy to obtain. Step-by-step directions, along with management tips, make it easy to guide students' investigations.

3. SCIENCE BACKGROUND AND VOCABULARY

Each activity includes a brief explanation of key concepts. You can adapt this information to meet the needs and abilities of your students. Periodically, key science words are defined in easy-to-understand language. Look for these in the margins.

4. CURRICULUM CONNECTIONS

Suggested curriculum connection activities in each center help you weave what you're doing in science with math, language arts, social studies, and art.

5. ASSESSING STUDENT LEARNING

This section features ideas for letting students demonstrate learning in a variety of ways. Another tool for assessing student learning is a science journal. Students can make their own by folding a 12-by-18-inch sheet of construction paper in half to create a folder, then adding paper. As students participate in each activity, they can record observations, thoughts, diagrams, and questions in their journals and add any Data Collection Sheets. Encourage students to revisit key concepts by taking time to look through earlier journal entries.

6. WINDOW ON CHILD DEVELOPMENT

You'll find tips in each center about how children might perform a skill or what you can expect them to understand. This information will be helpful as you plan your centers, activities, and assessments.

7. THINK ABOUT IT

How do you know if something is a seed? Why do you think birds have different kinds of beaks? Each center includes questions you can use to enhance children's windowsill center experiences. You can adapt both questions and answers to meet your students' needs.

8. EXTENDING THE ACTIVITIES

The suggestions here offer ways to expand students' learning. You might want to let children form cooperative groups to research areas of common interest. Encourage groups to share their discoveries with the class.

9. RESOURCES

This section suggests center-related books for children and teachers along with supply sources.

10. REPRODUCIBLES

These include Windowsill Science at Home activities, plus Data Collection Sheets for various investigations. Copy and send home page 8 at the start of your windowsill science explorations. Copy the others to have on hand as you set up new centers throughout the year.

When you're ready to start your windowsill science investigations, try Start-up Windowsill Science Center (see page 6), an activity that will boost students' observation skills—and inspire them to make new discoveries each time they look out the window.

START-UP WINDOWSILL SCIENCE CENTER

Like photographers looking through viewfinders to capture unusual shots, your students can use viewfinders they make to gain new perspectives on the world around them. *Zoom* by Istvan Banyai (Viking, 1995) makes a perfect introduction to this activity. In this unusual book, every turn of the page reveals a bigger part of a farm scene—beginning with a close-up of two children.

• • • • • • • • • •

MATERIALS

- ◉ *Zoom* (optional)
- ◉ blank, unlined 3-by-5-inch cards (one per student)
- ◉ colored construction paper (one sheet per student)
- ◉ white copy paper (one sheet per student)
- ◉ O-rings (optional)

STEPS

① As you read the book *Zoom*, ask students to predict what they will see on the next page. They will soon recognize that each successive page takes the reader one more step back from a scene. (If you don't have the book, start with step 2.)

② Have each student make a viewfinder by folding a blank index card in half and cutting a small window (about a 1-inch square) in the center of the card.

③ Let students use their viewfinders to focus on a scene outside the classroom window.

- ◉ Can students zoom in on one object?
- ◉ Can they hide that object from view and look at something else?
- ◉ How do they like their views if they crop out all the sky? If they include sky?

◉ Have students work in pairs to describe to their partners what they see inside their frames. Can they guess what their partners are describing?

④ Next, have each student glue the viewfinder to the center of an 8 1/2-by-11-inch piece of colored construction paper. Show how to cut out the area of construction paper that is inside the window of the card.

⑤ Have students place the construction paper on top of a plain white sheet of copy paper, then glue or staple the two sheets together along the left side.

⑥ Before going any further, ask children to share what they saw outside. When everyone has had a chance to contribute, ask children to draw parts of something that they saw inside the framed area of white paper, then lift the top sheet and draw more of the picture.

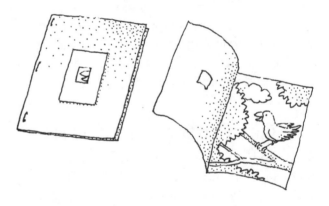

⑦ Bring students together in a sharing circle, letting them display their framed views and inviting classmates to guess what they are looking at. Notice whether students were able to capture the idea of looking at just part of something and how well related their guesses are to the parts of pictures they observe. You may also want to compile students' drawings into a class big book by punching holes in the margins and attaching O-rings.

ADDING A YEAR-ROUND FOCUS

In addition to the eight windowsill science centers featured in this book, weather is a natural topic to explore. Because weather is something children can observe on a daily basis, it makes a perfect year-round focus. With a few simple pieces of equipment, such as thermometers and rain gauges, you can turn your windowsill into a weather station where students can collect and record observations about the sun, clouds, precipitation, wind, temperature, and more.

WEATHER JOURNAL

Provide a weather journal at the windowsill for students, designating different teams to record the information each day. As children gather and record data, they'll build a wonderful resource for making all kinds of connections, such as creating graphs, recognizing patterns, and developing weather vocabulary. Suggestions for daily weather activities follow.

- Use pictures and/or words to describe the day's weather.

- Record the daily temperature (at the same time each day).

- Use pictures and/or words to describe the clouds today.

- Make a prediction for tomorrow's weather.

WEATHER WORDS

Be prepared to introduce new weather words to your students as the weather indicates. For example, if the weather reporter says, "There may be *gusts* up to 40 mph tomorrow," help students to discover just what a gust is. Or if the forecast includes rain, find a book like Franklyn Branley's *It's Raining Cats and Dogs: All Kinds of Weather and Why We Have It* (Houghton Mifflin, 1987) and share it with students. Another good book is *Weather Words and What They Mean* by Gail Gibbons (Scholastic, 1990).

Add to your year-round focus on weather by inviting students to make a Weather Words Dictionary. Begin by brainstorming a list of weather words, using their weather journals as reference. Students can alphabetize the list, then choose weather words to define and illustrate. Bind pages in alphabetical order with a couple of O-rings. Label one page *A*, the next *B*, and so on through the alphabet. As students learn new words, they can create new pages and insert them in the appropriate places.

Windowsill Science at Home

Dear _____,

We've set up a windowsill science center in our classroom to explore weather, investigate light, observe birds, grow gardens, and more. In the process, your child will be strengthening lifelong skills such as observing, classifying, predicting, comparing, making conclusions, and communicating. You can help your child build on some of these skills with this activity.

- Ask your child to look out a window and draw a picture of the view in Window 1. Label the season.

- In the next three windows, invite your child to draw pictures of how the view might change in the next three seasons. Again, label the seasons.

- Follow up by discussing changes your child expects to see. For example, how does a tree in summer compare with a tree in winter?

- Put this activity page on your refrigerator. As the year passes, help your child compare predictions with seasonal changes.

Window 1
Season: _____

Window 2
Season: _____

Window 3
Season: _____

Window 4
Season: _____

Bird Detectives

 When you work with students to make and hang up bird feeders, you will do more than provide food for feathered friends. You will also be providing food for thought for your students. Children are great observers and will be quick to notice that there is much diversity among birds. As children observe birds at their feeders, they'll have many opportunities to pay close attention to details: the shape and size of birds' bills, the way they eat, the way they move, the colors of their feathers. These details will help students learn more about how all birds are alike and how one species differs from another. Bird-watching is also a wonderful way to enhance children's awareness and appreciation for the animals that share our world.

PROCESS SKILLS: *observing, predicting, classifying, communicating, comparing, collecting and recording data, making conclusions*

ACTIVITY 1

Making Bird Feeders

Here are two simple bird feeders your students can create by recycling some everyday items. As students prepare their feeders, they can put research skills to work by learning more about the kinds of birds common to their area: What are they and what bird food do they favor?

Modification: *The best way for students to observe birds up close is to set out bird feeders near your classroom windows. If this is not possible at your school, investigate other nearby*

Birds who prefer insects, such as the phoebe, often migrate for the winter. Some birds have adapted their diets and will eat food that is available. When people make food easily accessible, they help birds conserve energy in months when food may be difficult to find. (When birds can find food easily at feeders, they expend less energy. This extra energy may help them survive extreme weather conditions.) Different birds prefer different kinds of food. For example, cardinals like sunflower seeds, cracked corn, and bread crumbs. Woodpeckers like suet. Be sure to keep feeders full in the winter since birds may come to depend on them as a reliable food source.

locations, such as a tree near the play area or the school entrance. If you are on a ground floor, you might also think about purchasing an inexpensive feeder that attaches to a window with suction cups.

MATERIALS (Hanging Bird Feeder)

For each group:

- clean, plastic one-liter soda bottle with cap
- masking tape
- string
- plastic lid (lightweight, such as those from margarine tubs; diameter should be larger than the bottle bottom)
- piece of paper
- birdseed
- Data Collection Sheet (see page 17)

For teacher use only:

- knife (such as an X-Acto or mat-cutting knife)
- permanent marker

Note: *Prepare the liter bottles by cutting out two triangles from each as shown. To do this, first punch three holes, equally spaced (about 1/2 inch apart), around the shoulder of the bottle. Use a knife to transform these holes into small triangles. This is where the seed will come out. Depending on the age of your students, you may also wish to prepunch holes for threading the string from which the feeders will hang. (See step 3.) To do this, punch two holes 1/4 inch above the plastic bottom of the bottle, on opposite sides.*

STEPS

① Before making the feeders, discuss how bird feeders help birds. (See Science Background, left.)

② Divide students into groups of three. Provide each group with a set of materials: liter bottle, masking tape, plastic lid, birdseed, paper, bottle cap.

③ Ask each group to complete the following tasks:

- Cover the triangular cutouts with masking tape. (This seals them shut and keeps seed from falling out until students are ready to hang the feeder.)

- Thread a piece of string, about 19 inches long, through the two holes in the bottle. Knot the ends.

- Trace around the cap of the liter bottle on the center of the lid. (You will then need to cut out the cap outline for

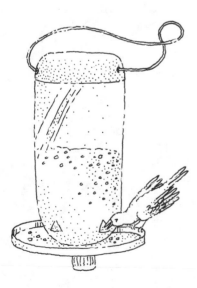

each group to make a hole in the plastic lid.)

- Push the neck of the bottle through the opening in the lid. Make sure that it is a snug fit.
- Use the paper like a funnel to add birdseed to the bottle. Screw the bottle cap on tightly.

④ When you're ready to hang the bird feeders outside, look for branches that will not be readily accessible to squirrels. Hang up the feeders and remove masking tape.

⑤ Let students observe the feeders daily, recording what they see on the reproducible Data Collection Sheet. (Each group can keep one or students may keep their own.)

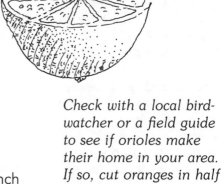

MATERIALS (Suet Balls)

- suet (this is beef fat that is available in the meat department of most grocery stores)
- double boiler
- birdseed
- cornmeal
- bread crumbs
- empty coffee can
- mesh bags (like the ones onions come in; cut into 5-inch squares)
- string (cut into 8-inch pieces)

Check with a local bird-watcher or a field guide to see if orioles make their home in your area. If so, cut oranges in half and set them out. Orioles love oranges!

Note: *Prepare the suet for this activity by cutting it into chunks and melting in a double boiler over low heat. Let the suet cool for a while (but not solidify again) before letting students begin.*

STEPS

① Let students add seed, cornmeal, and bread crumbs to the melted suet, using a spoon to mix.

② Carefully pour the mixture into an empty coffee can. Let cool until mixture solidifies. (You may wish to use this time to discuss with students how the suet changes its appearance as it is heated, and again as it cools.)

③ Give each student a 5-inch square of mesh-bag material and a scoop of the suet mixture. Let them mold the suet into balls and wrap in the mesh. Demonstrate how to pull the mesh together at the top, twist, and tie off with string.

④ Hang suet feeders in groups from tree branches where students can watch the birds feed.

SAFETY TIP!

Remind children not to put their hands in their mouths while handling the suet mixture. After completing the activity, make sure all children wash their hands with soap and water.

Get a feeling for students' attitudes toward other living things by inviting them to draw pictures or write sentences that show how they feel about caring for birds and other wildlife.

ACTIVITY 2

Observing Birds

Now that birds have started showing up at your windows, you can focus students' attention on the details they observe. With just a few details per bird, students can begin to recognize the diversity among birds. While students will recognize that they share some similar characteristics, they will also see how bird species differ.

MATERIALS

- dark paper
- masking tape
- chart paper
- two different color markers
- Data Collection Sheet from Activity 1

Note: *Birds have excellent vision and hearing. This may sometimes make it difficult for students to stand right up at the windows to observe the birds closely. Covering a window immediately in front of the feeders with dark paper will help provide a sort of buffer between bird-watchers and birds, and allow children to spy some great bird behaviors. Cut several slits in the paper so that students can look through. If possible, make binoculars available, too.*

STEPS

1. Tell students that they have just become members of the Great Bird Detectives Agency. It is their mission to try to find information that will help them find answers to some questions. Next, write the following questions on a piece of chart paper:

   - What colors are the birds we see from the window?
   - Do all the birds you see from the windows visit the feeders?
   - Do you think different birds prefer different kinds of food? Why?
   - Do the birds you see eat at the feeders or take the food and eat it somewhere else?

◉ What are some ways the birds you see move?

Hang the questions on the paper already attached to the window, above the student viewing holes.

② Make a set of these questions for students to keep in their science journals. Invite students to add their own questions, too. Have children record any information they find that pertains to the questions in their journals. Call together a weekly meeting of the Great Bird Detectives Agency to share information. Record new observations on the large chart posted at the window, using a different color marker than used for the questions.

● ● ● ● ● ● ● ● ●

Assessing Student Learning Before students start observing birds at their feeders, ask each to draw a picture of a bird and to write or dictate a sentence about the drawing. Collect these and set them aside. Later, after students have done plenty of bird-watching, ask them to repeat the above task. Compare their drawings and statements and note any changes in their drawings and sentences. Are they noticing more details that show what makes a bird a bird? Do they note differences between birds or describe bird behaviors?

CURRICULUM CONNECTION: Building Binoculars (Art)

Bathroom tissue tubes can become binoculars that students can use to focus on birds. Each child will need two tubes and a 2-foot-long piece of string. Have children place the tubes side by side and tape together using masking tape. Help students punch two holes on the outside edges of their tubes, then knot one end of the string through each hole. Students can decorate their binoculars using colored markers and stickers.

ACTIVITY 3

Flying Lessons

Help students discover the inspiration for inventing airplanes— birds! In performing this simple experiment, students will gain an understanding of the concept of *lift*, which allows both birds and airplanes to stay aloft.

lift:
the force that helps keep flying things aloft, or in the air

MATERIALS

- three pieces of copy paper

STEPS

① A day or two before this activity, ask your students to observe birds as they fly. Encourage them to record their observations in science journals.

② The day of the activity, if you have younger students, invite them to move like birds. Have them demonstrate how birds flap their wings, how they glide and soar, and even how they land. Older students can brainstorm a list of action words describing bird flight.

③ Next, read *Catching the Wind* by Joanne Ryder, a book that puts the reader in the role of a goose as it flies. (See Resources.)

④ Ask students to list similarities between a bird and an airplane. What part of both of these things helps them fly? (the wings)

⑤ Now use the copy paper to demonstrate the importance of wings. First, crumple one piece into a ball. Leave the second piece flat. (Set the third piece aside for now.) Explain that you are going to drop the papers at the same time from the same height. Ask them to predict which piece will reach the floor first.

⑥ After students make their predictions, hold both pieces above your head, then release. (The flat sheet will drift back and forth and will reach the floor after the crumpled piece.)

⑦ Ask students to try to explain what they just observed. What do they think allowed the flat piece to stay aloft longer? (As the flat piece moves through the air, the air creates lift as it pushes around the paper. Air passing the crumpled paper meets with less resistance and is able to drop more quickly.) Help students make the connection that wings on a bird and an airplane do the same thing as the flat sheet of paper—the air has to push around the wing and in doing so creates lift.

⑧ Finally, fold the third piece of paper in half from top to bottom. Open the paper back up. Hold the folded piece and the flat piece of paper above your head. Ask students to describe how they think each piece will fall. Encourage them to explain their reasoning, then release both pieces at the same time. Compare the fall of the two pieces. (Folding the paper helps to equalize the air pressure moving past the paper and creates a more balanced flight.)

Invite students to apply what they've learned by working in groups to design wings that will stay aloft longest. Does the width or length make a difference? Compare results with research on birds. For example, the albatross has a 9-foot wingspan that helps it stay aloft for days at a time.

WINDOW ON CHILD DEVELOPMENT

When it comes to bird identification, even preschoolers are very adept at identifying the birds they see in their backyards. However, at this age, it is important to place the emphasis on the bird-watching experience, allowing children to enjoy the birds they see. Talk about the birds' colors, their bills, the way they move. Let children describe the birds to you. Some may even come up with their own names for birds. When children are actively involved in observing these bird visitors, introducing names such as cardinal and chickadee will be readily accepted.

THINK ABOUT IT

The questions that follow are just some that your students might already be asking. The explanations are intended for your use. You can adapt the information to best meet your students' needs.

Why do you think some birds leave for the winter and other birds stay all year? If you live someplace where the weather gets cold in winter, many birds will leave, or *migrate*, as winter approaches. Birds that migrate move on to places where they will be able to find food and survive. The birds that remain are ones that have adapted to the rigors of finding food in winter.

Why do you think birds have different kinds of beaks? The variety of beak (or bill) sizes and shapes is connected to the type of food each bird eats. Birds with heavy, strong bills, like the cardinal, crack open seeds they eat. Birds with slender, long bills, like nuthatches, use their bills to poke into trees and find insects.

Why do you think birds have different kinds of wings? If you look closely, you will see that birds' wings have different shapes. These shapes typically match the lifestyle of the bird. Woodpeckers and many other backyard birds have broad, rounded wings, designed for maneuvering through the wooded areas in which they live. Birds such as Canada geese have long, broad wings to help them glide.

Do you think all birds fly? Ostriches and penguins are both examples of birds that don't fly.

migrate:
when animals move from one place to another to find food and shelter

EXTENDING THE ACTIVITIES

- Younger students can be on the lookout for flying things, keeping a list of anything they observe that flies. Invite them to sort items on their lists in different ways and share their sorting rules with you and classmates.

- Older students can research the history of flight and develop timelines to illustrate the evolution of flying machines over time.

- For avid bird-watching students, consider joining Project Feederwatch, a national ornithological study. A bird-watching kit includes a data collection form, an educational poster, and a quarterly newsletter. For more information, call (800) 843-BIRD.

- Investigate the possibility of creating a habitat for birds on school grounds. Involve students in planning, design, and planting stages.

RESOURCES

For Children

The Audubon Society Pocket Guides: Birds (Knopf, 1986). These pocket-size guides include color photographs and a complete description of each bird. The text will be too difficult for young children, but they will enjoy looking at the photos. Check for the edition that matches your part of the county.

A Beach for the Birds by Bruce McMillan (Houghton Mifflin, 1993). Meet the least terns, an endangered species that summers on a beach in Maine. Discover how they build nests called *scrapes* from sand, what the call *zreep…zreep…zreep* means, and how they get their feathers in top condition for their long journey south.

Catching the Wind by Joanne Ryder (William Morrow, 1989). Follow the adventures of a Canada goose as it flies over the countryside.

Our Yard Is Full of Birds by Anne Rockwell (Macmillan, 1992). A child's backyard bird-watching discoveries.

Outside and Inside Birds by Sandra Markle (Bradbury, 1995). Simple text and clear photos explain how and why birds fly.

What Is a Bird? by Ron Hirschi (Walker, 1987). Birds are identified in flight, in sleep, and in various other activities. See also *Where Do Birds Live?*

For Teachers

National Audubon Society North American Birdfeeder Handbook by Robert Burton (Dorling Kindersly, 1992). Lots of great photographs of common feeder birds plus tips for attracting and feeding birds, and information about bird behavior. A great teacher resource.

Bird Detectives

Name_____

DATA COLLECTION SHEET

Date Birds Observed	Color	Beak Shape	Behaviors	Food Eaten

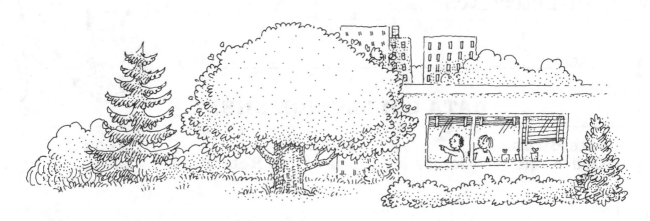

Shades of Green

Many thousands of different kinds of trees help make our world green. In this windowsill center students will observe trees outside their classroom windows, making discoveries about how the trees are alike and how they are different, noticing how they change with the seasons, and investigating how different structures help trees to survive.

PROCESS SKILLS: *observing, classifying, communicating, comparing, measuring, predicting, collecting and recording data, making conclusions*

ACTIVITY 1

I Spy a Tree

What makes the trees students see the same? What makes them different? In this game of I Spy, students enhance their observation skills and learn to differentiate between different types of trees.

deciduous:
trees, such as maples and oaks, that shed their leaves during autumn

evergreen:
trees that stay green all year; some, such as pines, have needle-shaped leaves; others, such as rhododendrons, have broad leaves

MATERIALS

two pieces of chart paper

marker

STEPS

① To play I Spy with students, first select a tree outside the classroom windows. Start by giving general clues about the tree. For example, "I spy a tree that is green."

② Write this first clue on one piece of chart paper.

③ Continue to offer clues until students guess the tree. Record each clue on the chart as you give it to your students. (You may wish to write clues ahead of time and keep them covered, revealing one clue at a time.)

④ Guide students in a discussion about the clues. Which clues apply to more than just the tree you selected? Which clues apply only to that one tree?

⑤ Have students compare how the trees they see are the same and how they are different. Draw a line down the middle of the second piece of chart paper. Label one side "same," the other side "different." Display the chart at the windowsill center. Add to it as students make more discoveries about the trees they see. Invite children to go further by experimenting with other ways to classify the trees. Create new charts to show their ideas.

• • • • • • • • • •

| Assessing Student Learning | Have students select two trees on their own. In their journals, ask them to write brief descriptions of the trees (including where they are located) and |

list three ways the two trees are the same and three ways they are different. (Children may also draw pictures to compare the trees.)

WINDOW ON CHILD DEVELOPMENT

Young children will often draw the same pictures the same way—over and over again. This kind of repetition provides a safety net for the child. Prior to participating in the activities at this windowsill center, young children may draw all of their trees the same—the standard lollipop-style tree. As students make closer observations of trees, you can encourage them to incorporate these new ideas in their drawings and help them grow not only in their understanding of trees, but in their own abilities as well.

ACTIVITY 2

Portrait of a Tree

Together, students select one tree for a long-term study and discover through their observations that a tree may have many different looks throughout the year. Keeping a class journal about the tree will allow children to look back at the tree over time, make comparisons, and expand their observations.

• • • • • • • • • •

MATERIALS

- ◉ *Sky Tree*, optional (see Resources)
- ◉ chart paper

- marker
- camera, film

STEPS

① If possible, share the book *Sky Tree*, written and illustrated by Thomas Locker, with students. In his author's note, Locker writes: "I have spent most of my life learning to paint trees against the ever-changing sky. I still cannot look at a tree without being filled with a sense of wonder." In a combination of science and art, Locker shares this wonder in *Sky Tree*. You may wish to read only one or two pages a day, allowing students time to explore how the author/illustrator portrays one tree.

② Let your students decide on one tree that they would like to observe. Explain that students will study this one tree as a class for the entire school year.

③ Take a photograph of the tree, noting the date. Attach this photo to a piece of chart paper. (This chart will serve as a class journal.) Next to the photograph, record the date of the photo. Let students collaborate to write a description of the tree on that date. Record this description on the chart paper under the date.

④ Try to have students observe the tree at different times during the day and under different weather conditions. Once a week, add a class entry to the journal. You don't always need to take a photo, but try to include one periodically.

⑤ After a month or two, reintroduce students to *Sky Tree*. Have them list the different conditions under which the author/illustrator observed this tree (in a soft summer breeze, in a cold wind, early one frosty morning, on a gray day, under a cloud-filled sky, and so on). Invite students to add other possibilities.

⑥ Using the class journal, *Sky Tree*, and their own experiences as reference, invite each student to illustrate the class tree under one of the conditions listed. Take time out to share "Connecting Science and Art in *Sky Tree*" (Thomas Locker's notes in the back of the book) to inspire students to experiment with color to create a mood. (For example, the artist creates a "hopeful" mood in The Bud Tree by using soft yellows to show the sun's warmth and fresh pinks and greens to represent spring.)

⑦ Compile students' tree portraits into a classroom book using O-rings (or punch holes, place in a three-ring binder, and decorate the cover). Invite students to add more portraits throughout the year if they wish.

• • • • • • • • •

| Assessing Student Learning | As students create moods for their tree portraits (see step 6), talk with them about how they might portray the tree. What are some ways to capture |

changes in daily weather or the seasons? Talk with students about the colors they might use for a snowy, rainy, or cloudy day. A cold day in autumn? How would their tree look in an early-morning mist? These conversations between you and your students will help them solidify their ideas and will help you determine how much each child understands about how the tree's appearance and its environment may change with the weather and seasons.

CURRICULUM CONNECTION:
Tree Roots (Social Studies)

Students can research and write histories for their tree, beginning with the tree's origins and what was happening at that time. For example, if students are studying a maple, they'll want to find out what a maple seed looks like and describe it. Students can also determine the approximate age of the tree. If the tree isn't too big, you may be able to find someone around school who can remember when it is was planted or how long ago the tree was a seedling. Share a copy of *The Big Tree*, by Bruce Hiscock, as an example of one tree's history. (See Resources.)

Autumn Leaves (Language Arts)

In the poem "Autumn Leaves," Aileen Fisher invites children to wonder what trees do "to make their leaves turn red and gold… instead of pink and blue." Ask young children to imagine leaves turning other colors, too. Write the poem on chart paper. (You can find it in *Out in the Dark and Daylight* by Aileen Fisher, [Harper-Collins, 1980].) Cut sentence strips to fit over the words *pink and blue,* then bring children together to read the poem. Ask them to think of other colors they'd like to see leaves turn, such as pink with polka dots. Children might enjoy decorating a craft-paper tree with leaves painted in these new colors. Display the poem nearby.

| Assessing Student Learning | Ask students to write a letter to a friend or relative describing the changing leaf colors of trees they see around school and their homes. |

Evergreen Explorations

Students discover how the leaves of an evergreen help the tree to conserve moisture and withstand harsh weather conditions.

SCIENCE BACKGROUND

Look closely at evergreens and you will notice a couple of things about their leaves—most seem to have a waxy covering and are thin and needle-shaped. Evergreens developed these adaptations to help them retain moisture. During times of freezing cold temperatures or dry conditions, evergreen leaves resist drying out. You can look at a rhododendron to get an idea of just how cold it is outside. The lower the temperature drops below freezing, the tighter the rhododendron's broad leaves will curl, helping it to retain moisture. (The leaves will also curl during dry spells in the summer for the same reason.) Though leaves on deciduous trees fall off, this is also a survival adaptation. When the leaves fall off, the food-making process shuts down, helping the trees conserve energy for the winter.

MATERIALS

For each group:

- two paper towels
- one sheet of waxed paper (same size as the paper towel)
- two paper plates
- water
- Data Collection Sheet (see page 25)

Note: *In this experiment, moistened paper towels represent leaves of different trees. One paper towel, wrapped in waxed paper, represents an evergreen tree leaf. The other, moistened but not wrapped in waxed paper, represents a deciduous tree leaf. Introduce this experiment by displaying samples of leaves from both evergreen and deciduous trees. Let children touch and compare the leaves. (If you can't supply actual leaves, try to provide photos of both kinds of leaves.)*

STEPS

1. Explain to students that they will be working in groups to find out how leaves help trees live. Invite them to share their own ideas about this.

2. Ask each group to:
   - wet the paper towels, then squeeze out excess moisture;
   - lay one paper towel flat on a paper plate;
   - lay the other paper towel flat on waxed paper, roll it up (with the waxed paper on the outside), and place it on the second paper plate.

3. Ask students to predict what will happen to each paper towel if left out overnight. Let them record their predictions on the Data Collection Sheet, then set the paper towels aside for the night in a place that does not get direct heat (away from a heat source, for example).

4. Let children check their paper towels the next day and record their findings on the Data Collection Sheet. Finally, have them complete the section asking them to compare their paper towels with leaves on trees.

Let students work on completing the Data Collection Sheet in their groups. Then bring children together to discuss and compare their results. (The one not wrapped in waxed paper, representing the deciduous tree leaf, should have dried out first.) Listen to students' explanations of their results. Can they make the connection between the two paper towels and the kinds of leaves they represent? If student' results are not the same, ask what they think might cause the differences. (Talk about factors that may have affected results, such as: Were both paper towels equally moist? Were they both set in the same place, away from heaters or other direct heat?) Repeat the experiment. But this time, control these factors.

THINK ABOUT IT

The questions that follow are just some that your students might already be asking. The explanations are intended for your use. You can adapt the information to best meet your students' needs.

Why do you think trees are important to us? Trees give us shelter, providing us with shade to withstand heat and wood to build homes. Other animals, such as squirrels and owls, make their homes in trees. Some, such as beavers, use wood from trees to build their homes. Trees also help to supply oxygen to our atmosphere. They provide beauty and inspiration in our world.

In what ways do you think a deciduous tree is like an animal that takes a long nap in the winter? As winter approaches and temperatures drop, the leaves on a deciduous tree slowly separate from the tree and die. When the weather warms up, new leaves appear. Losing its leaves actually helps a deciduous tree to survive the winter. With the leaves still on, the tree would be prone to losing a lot of moisture (through the leaves). By dropping its leaves, the tree retains more moisture, which helps protect the tree from drying up and dying. Like trees, some animals enter a period of dormancy when temperatures drop, allowing them to conserve energy when food supplies are scarce.

Do you think evergreens ever lose their leaves? Why? Yes. Individual evergreen leaves eventually die. Depending on the species, needles can live from 2 to 25 years. The leaves don't all die off at the same time, though, so while you will see brown needles that have fallen off, the tree, if healthy, will still be fully covered with green.

Do you think trees can grow anywhere in the world? Why? To grow, trees need at least eight inches of rain annually and a summer temperature of at least 50°F. Trees are not found growing high in the mountains or in Antarctica or the Arctic tundra.

EXTENDING THE ACTIVITIES

- ◉ Students might be interested in creating a field guide of trees around their school. Share it with the school library.

- ◉ Think about planting a tree on school grounds and caring for it. Tending a tree (or any other living thing) is a good way to encourage responsibility and a caring attitude for Earth. (See Resources for information about an inexpensive tree-planting kit.)

- ◉ Let students research an individual species of tree, including its physical description, what kind of seed it has, how the seed travels, possible uses as a natural resource, and history.

RESOURCES

For Children

The Big Tree by Bruce Hiscock (Aladdin Books, 1994). The life and times of a maple tree is traced from its days as a seedling during the American Revolution to its place of honor on a family farm 200 years later.

Discovering Trees by Douglas Florian (Aladdin Books, 1988). An introduction to trees that includes descriptions of different species, explanations of their life cycle, procedures for telling a tree's age, and ways we use trees.

Sky Tree by Thomas Locker (HarperCollins, 1995). Beautiful oil painting illustrations and simple, descriptive text portray one tree's changes throughout the seasons—fluttering in a soft summer breeze, losing its leaves on frosty autumn days, sleeping until spring, uncurling its leaves in the warm spring sun. Thoughtful questions invite the reader to connect the relationship between the artwork and the science. A special section in the back of the book shares the artist's techniques in creating the colors and mood of each illustration.

Trees and Forests by Gallimard Jeunesse (Scholastic, 1993). Reusable vinyl stickers, transparent and cutaway pages, and other special effects enhance the reader's exploration of trees. Topics include forests around the world, four seasons in the forest, and the relationship between people and trees.

Trees: A Golden Guide Book by Herbert Zim (Golden Press, 1952). Easy-to-use, pocket-size field guide of North American trees.

Why Do Leaves Change Color? by Betsy Maestro (HarperCollins, 1994). Children will enjoy looking at the different shapes and colors of leaves while learning why some trees change color in the fall, then lose their leaves. The very last page of the book includes places to visit for brilliant fall foliage viewing.

For Teachers

Picture Guide to Tree Leaves by Raymond Wiggers (Watts, 1981). Use the colorful close-ups of tree leaves to help children identify trees they see.

Supplies

Tree planting kits: Available from Weyerhaeuser (a paper company). Each kit contains a planting pot made from recycled paper, seeds, and an information booklet. For more information, call (206) 924-2345.

Shades of Green

Name_____

Names of others in my group

_____   _____

_____   _____

DATA COLLECTION SHEET

	Waxed Paper	No Waxed Paper
Which paper towel do you think will dry out first? Why?		
Which paper towel dried out first? Why?		
Which paper towel is most like a leaf on an evergreen tree? Why?		

Tiny Worlds

The activities in this center will help children gain a greater understanding of Earth's biosphere—by exploring tiny worlds on their windowsill.

Before beginning this center, you will need to think about obtaining several things. You will need pond mud and pond water for two of the activities. Maybe you have a pond near school that you could visit with students to collect what you need. If not, ask students if any of them live near ponds. Send a note home explaining what students are studying and asking parents to accompany their children to the pond to collect any samples. No pond mud and water nearby? Don't worry. You can easily make and substitute a hay infusion (see Activity 2).

You will also need at least one microscope for this center. A word about microscopes: they are available in a wide range of prices. There are a couple of different kinds that will work well on the windowsill. Brock Magiscopes are a favorite and utilize a clear lucite tube to collect light. They work great, need no batteries or electrical unit, and are nearly indestructible. But they are expensive—about $150 each. A great investment, but if you and your school are working on a tight budget, look at some of the smaller microscopes that use mirrors. Pocket microscopes are available for under $10. See Resources for more information.

PROCESS SKILLS: *observing, predicting, classifying, communicating, comparing, collecting and recording data, inferring, making conclusions*

ACTIVITY 1

Under a Microscope

Using microscopes gives children a chance to use the instruments scientists do to enhance their observations. In this activity, students make microscope slides to take a closer look at things they find.

biosphere:
the part of Earth and its atmosphere that supports life

From colors in comic strips to insects that have died, microscopes help children examine the structure of these things. (And as you'll quickly discover, they won't want to stop!)

. . . .

MATERIALS

- comic strip (or any other piece of colorful paper from a magazine or newspaper)
- paper lunch bags
- blank 3-by-5-inch cards
- transparent tape (the wider the better)
- microscope(s)
- Data Collection Sheet (see page 34)

STEPS

1. Introduce this activity by inviting children to take turns looking at a comic strip under the microscope. Before they look, ask: What do you think you'll see? When everyone has had a chance to look, have children compare their predictions with what they saw. (They'll see the structure of the colors—where they see orange in the comics, for example, they'll see yellow and red dots under the microscope. For more information, see Think About It, page 32.)

2. By now students will be eager to look at more samples. Talk about other kinds of things that will (or won't) fit under a microscope, then take a sample-collecting walk outside. Give each child a paper bag for collecting small samples, such as leaves, grass, flower petals, small pieces of tree bark, sand, dirt…essentially, whatever they can obtain a small sample of (without harming living things) that will fit inside their slides. Have students use their samples to make several slides each. (See How to Make Microscope Slides, right.)

   - Fold a 3-by-5-inch index card in half. Cut out a triangle on the fold. When you unfold the card, you'll have a diamond-shaped viewing window.
   - Place tape over the window on one side only. Place the sample on the sticky side. Cover the sample with tape.
   - Label each slide, identifying the sample, the person who made the slide, and the date.

3. Give students Data Collection Sheets. For each slide they look at, ask them to first draw what they think the sample will look like under the microscope. After viewing the sample under the microscope, ask them to draw what they actually see.

SCIENCE BACKGROUND
The lens of a microscope magnifies or enlarges objects by bending light. Light on its own travels in a straight line. The curve of the microscope lens causes the light to bend before it enters your eye, making the object appear magnified. The amount of magnification varies depending on the power of the microscope. A classroom microscope may magnify an object 30 times its actual size. Very powerful microscopes, such as those professionals use, can magnify images 100 million times the actual size.

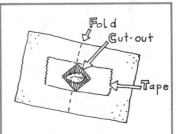

How to Make Microscope Slides
All you need to make slides are 3-by-5-inch index cards and some transparent tape. Demonstrate the procedure with students, then post directions for their own use.

④ Extend the activity by gathering a new assortment of samples. Make slides yourself, look at them, then draw large pictures of what you see. Number the drawings and assign each slide a letter. (Keep a record of how slide letters and drawing numbers match up.) Display the drawings, ask children to guess what each is, then have them take turns trying to match slides with drawings. Children might like to make their own slide-matching games to share with the class.

⑤ You'll probably find that the kids really enjoy making and looking at these slides. They will swap slides and eagerly share what they discover with their classmates. Encourage children to bring in other items from home, such as salt, pepper, tea leaves, cloth samples, onion skins, and so on. They'll discover there's a whole other world out there that they haven't ever seen! (Now, what will you do with all of these slides? See Curriculum Connection, below, for a class slide-filing system students can set up.)

• • • • • • • • • •

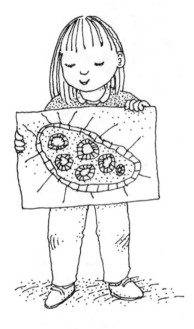

Assessing Student Learning Observe students' drawings of what they actually see under the microscope. Do the illustrations show detail that can only be observed using a microscope?

CURRICULUM CONNECTION:
Slide-Filing System (Language Arts)

After students make slides with their new samples, have them organize a classroom file, deciding on their own (or with guidance from you) how to sort and organize the slides. You may want to first group students to brainstorm possible systems, then bring the class together to share ideas and agree on an approach. (File boxes and shoe boxes work well for storing.) Store the file on the windowsill next to the microscope(s) so that it is accessible to students.

ACTIVITY 2

Making a Hay Infusion

The world around us is filled with life forms we don't ordinarily see. From bird baths and puddles to ponds and lakes, tiny plants and animals abound. Here, students use dried grass and rice to create a habitat for living organisms—in this case mostly protozoa, tiny one-celled animals like amoebas, paramecia, diatoms, and euglenas. They may also see other microscopic plants known as algae.

MATERIALS

- clear, quart-size jar with cover
- hay (a handful; any kind of dried grass from a field, empty lot, or yard will do)
- cooked rice (you'll need a few grains, any kind)
- pond mud, puddle water, stagnant water from a vase of flowers (any water in which life forms are already present, which is just about everywhere)
- eyedroppers
- microscope(s)
- microscope slides with covers (see Resources)
- cotton balls

STEPS

1. Put a small handful of dried grass in the bottom of the quart jar. Add several grains of cooked rice. If you want, add an inch or two of the pond mud. (This will add variety to the assortment of life in the jar.)

2. Fill the jar with water, then set on the windowsill, covered, for at least a week.

3. Ask students to write a brief description (and/or draw a picture) in their journals of what their pond in a jar looks like right after it has been put together.

4. One week later, let students take a sample out of the infusion using an eyedropper. Show them how to prepare a slide for the drop of water, following the directions here.

   - First wipe the slide with a cotton ball. (A few cotton fibers will help slow down the organisms in the water— the fibers get in their way.)

   - Gently squeeze out a drop or two of the pond water onto the slide. Cover the drop with a slide cover.

5. Place the slide under the microscope for viewing. Students can work in pairs so they can discuss their discoveries with a classmate. Have students draw what they see in their science journals. You might want to make several reference materials available so that students can try to identify the microscopic organisms they find. (See Resources for recommendations.)

6. How many different kinds of organisms do students think they spotted? What do they think their food sources are? Introduce food chains, guiding children to understand that all living things depend on other things for food.

SCIENCE BACKGROUND

In this experiment, bacteria grows on rice and hay, creating a feeding source for microorganisms. Some microorganisms will feed on the bacteria, some will feed on other microorganisms.

organism: a living thing—plant or animal; a microorganism is typically too small to be seen without the aid of a microscope

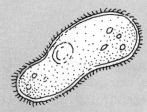

protozoa: single-celled organisms, usually microscopic

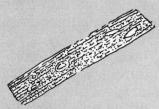

algae: a single-celled green plant

Let students form small groups to discuss their observations. As you visit each group, listen carefully to their conversations.

⦿ What words do students use to describe the organisms? Do they use size, shape, and color words?

⦿ How do they describe the way the organisms move?

⦿ What do they notice about changes in the jar ecosystem over time?

⦿ What are some of the ways they identify the organisms they saw? (By color, shape, size, and so on.)

⦿ What kinds of comparisons do students make in looking at one another's drawings? Do they notice new things?

CURRICULUM CONNECTION: Microscopic Movies (Technology)

Videomicroscopy equipment connects a microscope to a TV screen, allowing you to view tiny worlds captured under the microscope on the TV screen. Check with your school or district technology specialist to see if you have access to videomicroscopy equipment. You might also check with a local university science department or lab to see if they would be willing to demonstrate their equipment in your classroom—using students' pond slides.

ACTIVITY 3

Pond in a Jar

Bring a pond into your classroom to let students take a peek at life in that ecosystem and at the same time learn a little more about what makes Earth's other ecosystems work.

MATERIALS

⦿ clear, quart-size jar with cover

⦿ nail

⦿ candle wax

⦿ pond water and pond mud

⦿ snails, pond plants (optional)

⦿ microscope(s)

⦿ microscope slides with covers (see Resources)

⦿ eyedroppers

ecosystem:
the combination of plant and animal communities and their nonliving environment; in an ecosystem plants and animals interact with one another and with their environment (food chains are one example of how plants and animals interact with one another)

food chain:
a representation of the feeding relationships in an ecosystem where each organism depends on the next lowest member of the chain for its food; the chain begins with the sun, which provides energy for plants to grow

Note: *Before the activity, punch a hole in the lid with a nail. Seal the hole with melted candle wax. This sealed hole will help release any buildup of gases in the jar.*

STEPS

① Ask a couple of volunteers to fill the jar 3/4 full with pond water and add about an inch of pond mud. Add a few snails or plants to the jar if available.

② Ask students how this pond in a jar is like a real pond. Explain that like a pond ecosystem, this tiny pond has living organisms interacting with nonliving parts of the environment, like water or mud. Let students sketch the jar, noting the color of the water and any organisms they can already see. Ask children to record some predictions of what they think will happen in the jar.

③ Set the jar on the windowsill and have students continue to make and record observations over the next month or two. What changes do students see? What do they think is causing these changes? You may wish to take and examine a water sample from the jar every week or two to see if there is any difference in the population of organisms. (To do this, prepare a slide as in Activity 2, step 4.) As students gather information, discuss food chains. Where do they think the plants and animals in the pond get the food they need?

④ Enhance students' ability to think like scientists by inviting them to set up additional jars to investigate any of the following:

- comparing an ecosystem set up on the windowsill versus one set in a closet;
- introducing a pollutant such as a few drops of dishwashing liquid into the system;
- finding out whether water temperature affects the system;
- comparing pond water from different ponds;
- any other suggestions your students have.

• • • • • • • • • •

Assessing Student Learning | The best assessment is often based on the activities that are going on in your classroom. As students observe the pond in a jar, meet with them to talk about their journal entries for this activity. Or check journals periodically and record your own responses to inspire further observations and thought. Questions to guide journal assessment include:

- Do drawings reflect details, such as the size and shape of organisms?

The system that students create in the jar is much like the various ecosystems found on Earth. Like other ecosystems, there is a recycling of gases such as hydrogen, oxygen, and nitrogen within the jar. Sunlight comes through the classroom windows and enters the glass jar, providing energy as it does for other ecosystems. There are plants that utilize the sunlight to create food for themselves and for other organisms in the system. There will be consumers and decomposers that live off the energy of the plants. And as with any system, there will be changes over time.

- Do children record their predictions or make inferences based on their observations?
- Do students show increased use of details as the entries progress?
- Do students notice changes in the system over time?

CURRICULUM CONNECTION: Wiggle, Jiggle, Wriggle (Language Arts)

"In the small, small pond...wiggle, jiggle, tadpoles wriggle." *In the Small, Small Pond* by Denise Fleming is an appealing collection of action-oriented rhyming phrases featuring assorted pond inhabitants. (See Resources.) After sharing the book, invite students to create their own rhyming phrases for the organisms in their jar habitats (as a class, in pairs, or individually). You may even want to try creating books modeled on this pattern for a variety of other ecosystems, such as a field or forest.

WINDOW ON CHILD DEVELOPMENT

In the early elementary years children will begin to recognize the concept of a food chain. Most will understand that plants need sunlight to grow, that some animals eat plants and other animals eat plants and/or animals. You can use the reproducible Windowsill Science at Home activity to reinforce these understandings. Young children may have difficulty, however, comprehending that the plants make their own food. The concept of photosynthesis is best left for upper grades.

THINK ABOUT IT

The questions that follow are just some that your students might already be asking. The explanations are intended for your use. You can adapt the information to best meet your students' needs.

When you look at a comic strip under a microscope, why do you think you see tiny dots of color? The colors we see when we look at the comics are actually made up of tiny dots that we can't ordinarily see. When we look at the picture, our brains combine the dots to make new colors—such as orange, from red and yellow.

Why do you think the comic strips are not just printed with the colors the artist wants us to see? There are four colors in the printing process (magenta, yellow, cyan, black) that can be combined to make virtually every other color.

What are some ways you think microscopes are helpful to a scientist who studies soil or water? To a person who restores works of art? To a doctor? Microscopes help scientists break down what they are looking at so that they can see the smallest parts. This, for example, would make it easier for a scientist studying soil to see what is in the soil. It helps art restorers get all the details in a painting just right. It makes it easier for a doctor to tell what kinds of germs are making us sick.

How do you think the ecosystem in the jar is like the world we live in? See Science Background, Activity 3 (page 30).

Where do you think the plants and animals living in the jar get their food? The plants get their energy from the sun. The animals feed on plants and other animals.

EXTENDING THE ACTIVITIES

- Invite a doctor, scientist, art restorer, lab technician, or another person who uses microscopes to visit, bringing with them a high-powered microscope if possible. Let the visitor share how this tool helps with his or her work.

- In the jar pond, students were introduced to food chains. Let students investigate other food chains that exist locally, such as a field or stream.

- Older students can investigate what it is that allows Earth to support life while other planets in our solar system cannot.

RESOURCES

For Children

Hidden Worlds: Pictures of the Invisible by Seymour Simon (Morrow, 1988). This photo essay introduces children to the hidden worlds discovered under a microscope.

In the Small, Small Pond by Denise Fleming (Henry Holt and Company, 1993). A collection of action-oriented rhyming phrases to match a variety of pond inhabitants.

One Small Square: Pond by Donald Silver (Freeman, 1994). Take a closer look at life in a pond—and meet the extraordinary plants and animals that make their home in this ecosystem.

Pond Life: A Golden Guide by George Reid (Golden Press, 1967). This book may be pocket-size but it contains a wealth of information about a pond ecosystem, including different kinds of ponds, pond plants, one-celled organisms, insects, mollusks, reptiles, amphibians, and more. A terrific resource for all ages.

Supplies

Microscopes and slides
Delta Education, (609) 547-8880
Edmund Scientific, (800) 258-1302
Let's Get Growing, (800) 408-1868
or e-mail *letsgetgro@aol.com*
Nasco, (800) 558-9595

For Videomicroscopy equipment
The Scope Shoppe, (800) 577-2673

Tiny Worlds

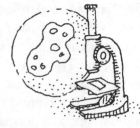

Name_____

DATA COLLECTION SHEET

Directions: For each sample you look at under the microscope, draw a picture of what you *think* you will see in Circle 1. Draw a picture of what you *do* see in Circle 2.

What I think I will see   **What I see**

Sample 1

[circle 1]   [circle 2]

Sample 2

[circle 1]   [circle 2]

Sample 3

[circle 1]   [circle 2]

You can use the back of this paper to draw more samples.

Evaporation Investigations

Jumping in puddles—it's fun while it lasts, but eventually those puddles disappear. In this windowsill center, students discover the reason and continue the fun as they create classroom puddles to explore the concept of evaporation. Students will have an opportunity to explore evaporation rates, discover how evaporation affects our daily lives, and think about just what happens to those puddles!

PROCESS SKILLS: *observing, communicating, comparing, measuring, collecting and recording data, inferring, predicting, making conclusions*

ACTIVITY 1

Where Does Water Go?

Students get acquainted with the concept of evaporation and discover the role it plays in the water cycle by observing two jars of water on the windowsill—one open and one closed.

MATERIALS

- identical clear containers
- measuring cup
- water
- permanent marker
- plastic wrap

evaporation:
the process by which water (a liquid) turns into water vapor (a gas)

water cycle:
the movement of water from clouds to Earth, then back to clouds again

A puddle is made up of water in its liquid state. As water molecules in a puddle heat up, they move faster and farther apart. This allows the water molecules to escape into the air. When this happens, the water molecules are no longer visible. At this point, water is changing from a liquid state to a gaseous state called water vapor. This is the process of *evaporation*.

Evaporation is just one part of the water cycle. As water evaporates and rises into the atmosphere, it cools and changes into water droplets. This is called *condensation*. Eventually these water droplets join together to fall back to Earth as rain, snow, or some other form of precipitation—then the cycle begins again.

STEPS

① Ask two students to fill the two containers with equal amounts of water. Invite a couple more volunteers to mark and date the water level on each jar with the permanent marker. Cover the top of one of the jars with plastic wrap.

② Ask students to predict what will happen to the water in each of the containers when left on the windowsill. Have students draw and label the two containers in their science journals, then record the date and their predictions.

③ Every three to four days, ask students to check the water levels in the jars, marking and dating new levels on the container if necessary. Each time they do a water-level check they can record the date and their findings in their science journals.

• • • • • • • • •

Assessing Student Learning After a couple of weeks, ask students to review their observations by looking back through their journals. What statements can they make about the water in the two jars? The water in the open jar seems to be slowly disappearing, or evaporating. Students may have noticed in the closed jar that water droplets form on the inside of the plastic wrap and along the sides of the jar. These drops fall back into the water, so the level of the water in the closed jar remains fairly steady.

ACTIVITY 2

Puddle Races

Students make (contained) puddles in the classroom and discover that the warmer the location of their puddles, the more quickly the puddles evaporate.

• • • • • • • • •

MATERIALS

- eyedroppers (one per team)
- baby food jar lids (two per team)
- water
- small cups
- chart paper
- permanent markers
- Data Collection Sheet (see page 42)

Note: *Students will be placing one of their puddles on the windowsill. The other puddle needs to be in a place that is cooler than the windowsill. You will want to decide on this location* *ahead of time, letting the students discover through the investigation the reason for the different evaporation rates.*

STEPS

① Begin the activity by sharing a book that introduces the concept of the water cycle. *Rain, Drop, Splash* by Alvin Tresselt or *The Water's Journey* by Eleonore Schmid do a nice job. (See Resources.)

② Let students work in teams of two for this activity. Explain that they are going to be making puddles in the classroom. Invite them to suggest some ways they could do this. Then share the materials and ask them how they think they could use two jar lids, an eyedropper, and a small cup of water to make puddles.

③ Demonstrate how to use an eyedropper to make a puddle on the lid of a baby food jar. Have children count the drops as you put them in. (The number of drops doesn't matter, though you will probably want at least five to ten.) Record the number of drops you put in the lid and post this at the center as a reminder. Ask children why they think it is important that they all use the same number of drops. (This is a good opportunity to discuss fair testing. By using the same number of drops in each lid, you eliminate the amount of water as a variable in comparing results.)

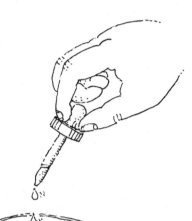

④ Have students write their initials on the inside of their lids, then use the eyedropper to make a puddle in each. Show students where to place their puddles (one on the windowsill, one in a cooler location that you predetermine). Have students label the second location on their Data Collection Sheets, then ask them to record their predictions: Which puddle will evaporate more quickly: the one on the windowsill or the one in (other location)?

⑤ Let students check their puddles every five minutes until one of the puddles completely evaporates, then complete their Data Collection Sheets.

⑥ Create a chart for compiling class results by writing the names of the two locations across the top. (Students will write their names down the left side.) Post the chart, then bring children together to share results. Let each pair of students record their names and put a check under the location of the puddle that evaporated first. When everyone has recorded their data, ask students what true statements can be made about the results. For example, "The puddle on the windowsill disappeared first for all the groups." Write these statements at the bottom of the chart paper. Note: The puddles in the warmer, sunnier locations should evaporate first. If this is not the case, discuss differences with students. Ask: Why do you think we didn't all get the same results? For example, students might wonder if everyone put in the same number of drops. Let children repeat the experiment, again charting and comparing results.

⑦ After students make statements about the results, ask them for possible explanations. Invite students to suggest ways to prove their explanations. Most likely, someone will suggest measuring the temperature of both locations. Provide students with thermometers to try this out.

• • • • • • • • • •

Assessing Student Learning The final question on the reproducible asks students to think of a way to make a puddle evaporate quickly. (Students might suggest setting the puddle on something warm, such as a heater.) After completing Activity 3, ask students if they can think of another way to make a puddle evaporate more quickly. Let students test out some of their ideas.

WINDOW ON CHILD DEVELOPMENT

Children's understanding of evaporation and the water cycle develop throughout the elementary years. Primary-age students will recognize that water in a puddle or in an open container disappears, but they will probably not understand that the water is still present as an invisible gas (water vapor). Understanding of these concepts is best learned by involving students in hands-on activities that allow them to make observations, collect information, and make conclusions about what happens to the water. By revisiting these concepts with related activities, you can build on students' prior understanding and enhance concept development.

ACTIVITY 3

Drying Laundry

In this activity, students build on what they have learned about evaporation rates by exploring and comparing other variables that can affect drying time.

• • • • • • • • • •

MATERIALS

- ● a piece of cloth, such as an old sheet, cut into 5-inch squares (two squares per group)
- ● clothesline
- ● clothespins
- ● hand lenses

wind: moving air

absorbent: soaking up of water

- tub (or sink) of water
- masking tape
- chart paper
- marker

Note: *For the purposes of this activity, students will need access to a window that will open. If this is not possible, investigate other locations in the school, or replace the open window in the experiment with a fan (to represent moving air).*

STEPS

1. Before the activity, hang a clothesline in the window of your windowsill center. Clip clothespins on the line.

2. Break the class into small groups. Give each group two cloth squares. Ask students to use the hand lenses to take a close look at the cloth. You can also have children view the cloth under a microscope, reminding them of the Tiny Worlds activities. (See page 26.) Ask them to use pictures and words to record observations in their science journals, including the weave of the cloth.

3. Have students set their squares in a container of water. While the cloth soaks, review the idea that increased temperatures make water evaporate more quickly. Ask students if they know of other ways to make something dry more quickly. Students may suggest fanning their cloth squares as a way to speed up evaporation. Ask: How do you think moving air (wind) will change the drying time of your fabric squares?

4. Let each group retrieve two of the wet cloth squares and squeeze out the excess water. Have them hang one square in front of an open window and the other square in front of a closed window.

5. Let students periodically check their laundry and record which square dries out first. Bring students together to discuss results. What conclusions can students make about the conditions that are best for drying laundry?

6. The clothesline can become a semipermanent addition to your windowsill center, lending itself to many more evaporation investigations. For example, students can test and compare drying times of different kinds of materials or drying time with temperature. The possibilities are limitless.

• • • • • • • • •

| Assessing Student Learning | Let students work together in their groups to brainstorm ways that people evaporate water every day (hair dryers, clothes dryers, clotheslines, and so on). |

SCIENCE BACKGROUND
In addition to heat, evaporation rates can also vary due to the amount of humidity and wind. Clothes on a line will dry fastest on a warm, dry, breezy day. The type of fabric can also affect drying time. Lightweight items such as sheets absorb less water and will dry faster than heavier, more absorbent pieces, such as sweatshirts.

As students share their ideas, listen to see whether the devices they describe incorporate the concept of evaporation.

CURRICULUM CONNECTION: Berry Roll-ups (Social Studies, Math)

Before refrigeration, people preserved food by drying it. For example, sailers packed fish and beef in salt to preserve it for long voyages. Challenge students to apply what they've learned in other activities by inventing their own food preservers. Provide assorted materials such as boxes, aluminum foil (reflects heat back on the food being dried), tape, string, cheescloth (will keep fruit free from bugs), as well as fruits such as grapes and apples. If you'd like to dry fruit as a class, here's an easy recipe for fruit leather.

MATERIALS

- 4 cups strawberries (or any edible berry)
- bowl
- potato masher
- cookie sheet
  - cheesecloth (optional)
  - waxed paper

STEPS

1. Place the berries in the bowl, and mash.

2. Spread the mashed berries out evenly on the cookie sheet. Cover with cheesecloth if desired.

3. Let the mashed berries dry. (This will take a couple of days.) Invite children to select a spot, based on investigations in this and other centers, that they think will speed up evaporation.

4. When the mashed berries are dry, cut into strips and let children eat them or roll them up in waxed paper to save.

THINK ABOUT IT

The questions that follow are just some that your students might already be asking. The explanations are intended for your use. You can adapt the information to best meet your students' needs.

Why are there puddles when it rains? As rain falls, it collects in lower-lying areas of sidewalks, roads, parking lots, and backyards. If the surface on which the water falls is very hot, such as on the pavement of a parking lot, the puddle may not get much of a chance to form as it will evaporate more quickly.

Where does the water from a puddle go? As the water in the puddle evaporates, the now invisible water vapor rises into the atmosphere. Eventually, this same water vapor cools and condenses into a liquid again, in the form of droplets. When many of these droplets join together the result is a cloud.

Why doesn't the ocean dry up? Thanks to the water cycle, large bodies of water are constantly replenished. But here is another question: Why doesn't the rain taste salty? (Salt doesn't evaporate with the water. Children might like to test this.)

EXTENDING THE ACTIVITIES

- Before a rainfall, let students predict where puddles will form. Mark predicted puddle perimeters with chalk or string and then watch to see where puddles form. Children can also outline puddles that form, then observe what happens as the water evaporates.

- Let students explore water in its three states (solid, liquid, gas). Can they think of ways to take a cup of water (liquid) and change it into a solid? (Place in freezer.) Into a gas? (Heat it up.)

- Invite students to find out how changes in the water cycle affect our weather.

RESOURCES

For Children

It Could Still Be Water by Allan Fowler (Children's Press, 1992). Simple photos and text show the different forms water can take.

Rain, Drop, Splash by Alvin Tresselt (Lothrop, Lee and Shepard, 1946). Poetic text and illustrations follow raindrops as they make a puddle, which leads to a lake, then a river, and eventually an ocean.

The Water's Journey by Eleonore Schmid (North-South Books, 1995). Clear text and illustrations of landscapes explain the water cycle for young readers.

For Teachers

Where Puddles Go by Michael Strauss (Heinemann, 1995). A terrific resource with activities and explanations about concepts associated with the water cycle and other physical changes.

Supplies

Eyedroppers
  Edmund Scientific, (609) 547-8880
  Delta Education, (800) 258-1302

Evaporation Investigations

Name_____

DATA COLLECTION SHEET

	Puddle Location 1: Windowsill	Puddle Location 2:
My Prediction		
Which puddle evaporated first?		

Why do you think this happened?

Can you think of another way to make a puddle evaporate?
On the back of this paper, draw a picture to show your idea.

The Way Light Works

In the activities here, students will investigate rainbows and explore shadows to discover some of the properties of light. When you are ready to introduce this windowsill center, hang one or two rainbow-making crystals in your classroom window. (Check flea markets for old chandelier crystals.) Your students will really love the way these scattter rainbows around the room.

PROCESS SKILLS: *observing, predicting, classifying, communicating, comparing, collecting and recording data, making conclusions*

ACTIVITY 1

Making Rainbows

Here, students experiment with a few simple materials to create rainbows in the classroom. By repeating the experiment and by comparing results with one another, students will discover that the order of colors in a rainbow is always the same: red, orange, yellow, green, blue, indigo, violet (ROY-G-BIV).

MATERIALS

For each group:

- prism (see Resources)
- pocket-size mirror

SCIENCE BACKGROUND

Raindrops act as nature's prisms. Light, including sunlight, travels in straight lines. When these light rays are bent, as when they pass through a prism, a spectrum of beautiful colors called a *rainbow* results.

rainbow:
a band of colors
created by light
passing through
water (such as
sunlight passing
through raindrops)

- clear container (this doesn't have to be very big; just large enough to hold a pocket-size mirror)
- white poster board

STEPS

1. Have each group fill a container with water, then set the container on the windowsill in direct sunlight.

2. Demonstrate how to place a mirror in the water so it is facing the sunlight. Have each group do the same.

3. Show students how to adjust the angle of the mirror until you are able to cast a rainbow. You may wish to place a sheet of white poster board between the container and the window, making a surface on which to catch the rainbow. Let students experiment with their own mirrors to make rainbows.

· · · · · · · · · ·

Assessing Student Learning

Observe students trying to make their rainbows. Do they adjust the angle of the mirror? Ask students to use their science journals to describe their rainbows and to draw pictures of what they see. Do they draw the colors in the correct order?

ACTIVITY 2

Colors of a Rainbow

Children discover that they can mix three colors to create six, for a rainbowlike effect.

Note: *Before beginning this activity, cut red, yellow, and blue cellophane into 4-inch squares, one square per student. (Make sure that there are approximately the same number of red, yellow, and blue squares. For example, if you have 24 students, cut 8 squares of yellow, 8 squares of red, and 8 squares of blue.) Place cellophane squares in a bag.*

· · · · · · · · ·

SCIENCE BACKGROUND
Cellophane is pigmented. When children overlay one color with another, the colors appear to mix, creating a new color. Because cellophane is transparent, light will pass through easily, making the new colors easily visible.

MATERIALS

- red, yellow, and blue cellophane
- a brown paper lunch bag
- clear tape

STEPS

1. Introduce the activity by sharing *Colors* by Gallimard Jeunesse. (See Resources.) When you get to transparent pages that allow you to mix colors (by overlaying colors on

one page with colors on the transluscent page), let students first predict the resulting colors. For example, what color do they think they'll see when blue mixes with yellow?

② After reading the book, let each child pick a piece of the rainbow out of the paper bag.

③ Ask students to think back to the first activity. Ask: What colors do you see in a rainbow? How do you think we can make those colors from the colors we are holding?

④ Let students experiment with the color overlays to achieve the colors of a rainbow. (One way to do this is to tape the red cellophane on first, creating a line of red. Next, tape the yellow cellophane to the window, overlapping 1/2 inch with the red cellophane. Finally, add the blue cellophane, again overlapping 1/2 inch with the yellow cellophane. When light shines through the cellophane, a rainbow will form.)

• • • • • • • • •

| **Assessing Student Learning** | To help children recognize that the order of colors in a rainbow is always the same, invite them to compare the pictures of their rainbows from Activity 1 with their results in Activity 2. How are the rainbows the same? |

Shadow Graphs

Introduce children to light and shadows by exploring the way light passes through or is blocked by different objects.

Note: *Before the activity, cut a piece of cardboard, a piece of waxed paper, and a piece of clear acetate so that each measures approximately 5-by-5 inches. Tape them in a horizontal row to the wall or a chalkboard. Next, cut about twenty 2-inch squares from each of these materials.*

• • • • • • • • •

MATERIALS

- cardboard
- waxed paper
- clear acetate sheets (for overheads)
- masking tape

SCIENCE BACKGROUND

Light from the sun passes easily through transparent glass windows. In colonial times, windows were made from oiled paper, a translucent material. Light passing through these windows was scattered and fuzzy. When light rays hit an opaque object, the light can't pass through and thus casts a shadow of the object. Cardboard boxes, tree trunks, and even kids are examples of objects that can make shadows by blocking light.

STEPS

① Direct students' attention to the three pieces you have taped to the wall. Ask them to predict which of the three squares will make a shadow when placed in the sunlight.

② After giving them some time to think, let each student commit to a prediction by selecting a smaller square made from the same material.

③ Tape one of each of the smaller squares to the window in a horizontal row. (See illustration, page 45.) Let students graph their predictions by taping their squares to the window, one above another, in the column with the matching material. This will form a bar graph representing their predictions.

④ Ask children to notice which squares cast shadows into the classroom. (Hopefully, you will be doing this on a sunny day. But if you are not, leave the graph up until you do get one.) Which material (cardboard, waxed paper, clear acetate) makes shadows?

• • • • • • • • • •

Assessing Student Learning   Find out if your students understand the concepts in this activity by asking them to make lists of other materials that they think are opaque, transluscent, and transparent. Let them work in groups to test out their ideas. Cut out three speech balloons, one for each type of material, from chart paper and tape them to the windows. Let students record their discoveries on these speech balloons as they classify the items they test.

WINDOW ON CHILD DEVELOPMENT

When children sort and group objects, they are classifying. Over time, their classification schemes become more complex. While younger children will classify their objects simply as transparent, transluscent, or opaque, older students can organize their items in more detail. For example, they may arrange the items on a scale of most transparent to most opaque.

THINK ABOUT IT

The questions that follow are just some that your students might already be asking. The explanations are intended for your use. You can adapt the information to best meet your students' needs.

Where do you think the colors in a rainbow come from?
When light is bent and reflected back, it is always broken into the same spectrum of colors: red, orange, yellow, green, blue, indigo, violet.

Do the colors always appear in the same order? Yes. Colors always appear in the order of the lengths of each wavelength—from longest to shortest (red to violet).

What do you think would happen if you tried to make rainbows on an overcast day? One of the ingredients in rainbows is sunlight. On an overcast day, you wouldn't see rainbows.

How do you think changing the angle (position) of the mirror changes what you see? Depending on the angle of the light and how it is reflected back, you may or may not see a rainbow.

How do you think a rainbow gets its shape? When we see an arched rainbow in the sky, we are actually just seeing part of a perfect circle. The center of the circle is located below the horizon, leaving just a part of the circle visible to us.

EXTENDING THE ACTIVITIES

Children who show special interest in the way light works might like to explore related areas in greater detail. Some suggestions follow.

- Explore folklore related to shadows and rainbows.
- Investigate cloud rays and other light-related phenomena.
- Research careers that relate to color (such as artist, decorator, landscaper, quilter).

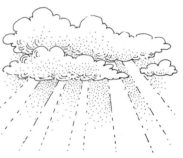

Cloud rays

RESOURCES

For Children

Colors by Gallimard Jeunesse (Scholastic, 1991). Part of the "First Discovery" series, this interactive book introduces children to the colors of the rainbow. With the turn of a transparent page they can turn yellow and blue to green, red and yellow to orange, and more.

Light by Gallimard Jeunesse (Scholastic, 1992). Another "First Discovery" title, this book introduces children to light—from colorful rainbows to the aurora borealis.

Shadow Magic by Seymour Simon (Lothrop, 1985). Pictures in this book demonstrate concepts associated with shadows. Includes some activities.

Shadowgraphs Anyone Can Make (Running Press, 1991). A simple guide to making shadow pictures.

For Teachers

Simple Science Experiments with Light by Eiji Orii and Masako Orii (Gareth Stevens Children's Books, 1989). Activities for exploring light and shadows.

Primarily Physics (AIMS Education Foundation). Thirty-two hands-on activities for exploring the concepts of sound, light, and heat energy.

Supplies

Inexpensive prisms
Delta Education, (800) 258-1302
Edmund Scientific, (609) 547-8880

Windowsill Science at Home

Dear _____,

We're learning about light in class. You can reinforce your child's understanding by trying this simple activity. Look out a window together after dark tonight. Talk about the lights you see. Which are examples of natural light (the moon, stars, fireflies)? Which lights are from objects made by people (streetlights, headlights, porch lights, lights from passing aircraft)? Record your discoveries on the chart. Ask your child to bring the chart back to school by _____.

Natural Lights	**Other Lights**

The Sun's Warm Ways

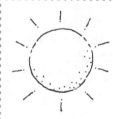

In The Way Light Works (see page 43), students discovered some properties of the sun's light. Here they explore the heat given off by sunlight. Naturally, you'll want to plan these activities for a sunny day.

PROCESS SKILLS: *observing, classifying, comparing, measuring, predicting, collecting and recording data, making conclusions*

ACTIVITY 1

Hot Spots

Students will observe the differences in temperatures where sunlight is present and where it is not as they explore the connection between light and heat.

SCIENCE BACKGROUND

Light, such as that from the sun, gives off heat. Heat is a form of energy. It is the absence or presence of heat that affects temperature—whether something is hot or cold.

● ● ● ● ● ● ● ● ●

MATERIALS

- shoe box
- two thermometers
- masking tape

STEPS

① Set the box upside down on the windowsill. Ask students to imagine that the box is a hill. Which side of the box do they

think is receiving direct sunlight? Which side is not? Encourage them to explain their choices.

② Have students pretend that they live on the side of the hill that is in direct sunlight and that they have a friend who lives on the other side. Is the temperature outside the same for them as it is for their friends on the other side or is it different? Again, let children explain their responses.

③ Next, ask students if they can think of a way to test the temperature on both sides of the hill. If students have been collecting data about the weather (see Adding a Year-Round Focus, page 7), they may be familiar at this point with using the thermometer as a tool to measure temperature. Discuss this approach and any other ideas before moving on to step 4.

④ Guide students to recognize that one way to test the temperature is to attach a thermometer to each side of the box. (You can use tape.) Let students record the initial temperature on both thermometers, then recheck the temperature on both sides of the hill (box) every 15 minutes for an hour. Record this information on a chart. (Older students can create their own charts to record data.)

⑤ After an hour, ask students to look at the data they collected. What conclusions can they draw about sunlight and temperature? (The side in direct sunlight will be warmer than the side that isn't receiving direct sunlight.)

• • • • • • • • • •

Assessing Student Learning Invite students to apply what they've learned in this group mapping activity. Have students work in groups to make maps of predicted hot spots and cool spots in the classroom. Which spots do they think will be the hottest? Coolest? Have students create simple maps of the classroom, then mark their predictions. Check their predictions to see if students recognize that hot spots will be located in areas of direct sunlight. (If you are doing this activity in the winter, students may predict that areas near heaters will be hot. This is okay. Just ask them to explain their reasoning.) Let students set out thermometers at the designated spots and measure the temperatures every 15 minutes or so for an hour. How does the data they collect compare with their predictions? Let students make new maps showing actual hot spots. (Or bring groups together to compile data and create a class map.)

Sunlight and Surfaces (Part 1)

Students explore the differences in the amount of heat absorbed by materials with different surfaces.

• • • • • • • • • •

MATERIALS

For each group:

- three small, clear plastic cups (all the same size)
- soil
- water
- sand
- three thermometers
- Data Collection Sheet (see page 57)

Note: *Set out the thermometers in advance of this activity, allowing them to adjust to room temperature. This will help each group begin the experiments at a similar starting temperature, so that they can later compare their results. (This may be a good time to discuss the concept of fair testing—in this case, having groups start at the same temperature to control the variable of temperature from one group to another.) Also, if you don't have enough thermometers, you can have groups take turns over a period of a few days.*

STEPS

① Divide students into groups. Give each group a set of materials.

② Have each group fill the three cups—one with water, one with soil, and one with pebbles or sand.

③ Ask students what they think will happen if they set the cups on a sunny windowsill. Discuss their responses. If no one has mentioned that the materials in the cups may heat up, suggest the possibility. (Review the results of Activity 1, in which students discovered that a spot in sunlight will be warmer than a spot that is not in sunlight.)

④ Next, ask students to predict which cup will collect (absorb) the most heat. Have them record their predictions in the space provided by checking the appropriate space.

⑤ Have each group check the initial temperature on the thermometers and record this information on the Data Collection Sheet. Students should then place the thermometers all the way in the cups. Discuss the reason for making sure the thermometers are placed the same way

SCIENCE BACKGROUND

Smooth and shiny surfaces, like that of water, reflect back much of the sun's light and, along with it, heat. Darker and rougher surfaces, like those of soil and pebbles and sand, collect or absorb more of the sun's light to produce heat. The same applies to colors. Black, the darkest color, absorbs the most sunlight, making it heat up more than white, the lightest color, which reflects back all of the sunlight and feels cooler.

heat:
the kind of energy that makes things feel hot or cool

heat absorption:
the taking up of heat from the sun's light by another substance

51

in each cup (again, the concept of fair testing).

⑥ Have students record temperatures for each cup after 30 minutes and after one hour, each time recording the temperatures on the Data Collection Sheet.

⑦ After the last temperatures are collected and recorded, let students in each group work together to make conclusions about the materials and their heat-absorption qualities. Bring groups together to share and discuss results. (Water is going to reflect a lot of the light back and will remain cooler. Soil will absorb the most heat because it has a darker surface.)

• • • • • • • • • •

Sunlight and Surfaces (Part 2)

Students build on what they learned about water, sand, and soil as they investigate the colors of the clothes they wear.

• • • • • • • • • •

MATERIALS

- construction paper (you will need at least one sheet of black and one sheet of white plus assorted other colors)
- thermometers (same number as sheets of construction paper)
- clothesline and clothespins
- masking tape

Note: *Before beginning this part of the activity, string a clothesline across the window area. Cut the construction paper into T-shirt shapes. Bring thermometers to room temperature.*

STEPS

① Ask students to imagine they are playing outside on a hot summer day. What are they wearing? Do they think the color of their T-shirts makes a difference in how warm they feel? Let them share their experiences, noting whether some students already associate the idea that darker colors absorb more sunlight and therefore feel warmer.

② Show students the clothesline. Explain that together you would like to set up an investigation to find out what color T-shirt will help them feel cooler while playing in the sun. Show them the two T-shirts you have already picked out to test (one sheet of white construction paper and one black) and request that they help you pick out four more shirts from the stack. At this point let your students vote on four more colors to add to the investigation. Let them help you cut the paper into T-shirt shapes, using the precut black and white ones as templates.

③ Involve children in creating a chart to record the data they collect. They might cut out tiny T-shirt shapes in each of the colors they're testing, glue them down the left side of the paper, then make three columns labeled "starting temperature," "after 30 minutes," and "after 1 hour."

	Starting Temp.	After 30 Min.	After 1 Hour

④ Help students use tape to attach thermometers to the back of each T-shirt, then record the initial temperature of each on the chart.

⑤ Together, check the T-shirt temperatures after 30 minutes and again after one hour. Record these on the chart.

⑥ Ask students to rank the T-shirts, from hottest temperatures recorded to coolest. Based on their findings, which color do they think would be most comfortable in warm weather? (The cooler the temperature the better. Generally, white is the coolest and black is the warmest.)

• • • • • • • • • •

Assessing Student Learning	Ask students to draw or write about the type of clothing, including color, they might wear if they were:

◉ playing in snow;

◉ playing softball at a summer picnic.

Let them share their choices with you, explaining how they made their clothing selections.

CURRICULUM CONNECTION ACTIVITY:
Sandpaper Prints (Art)

Students use the warmth of the sun in a simple printing process. Start by giving each student a piece of sandpaper. Let them use old crayons to color pictures on the sandpaper. Encourage them to press hard—something they'll enjoy doing! When they are finished with their designs, let them set the sandpaper pictures on the windowsill in direct sunlight. Ask: What do you think will happen to your pictures in the sunlight? Let them find out by observing how the waxy crayon gets sticky as it warms up. When the pictures are warm, let students press plain white paper over the top of the sandpaper and gently rub without moving the paper. When students peel off the paper, they'll have prints of their designs to display around the windowsill center.

Keeping Heat Out

Students explore the insulating properties of different materials and decide which ones do the best job of maintaining temperature.

• • • • • • • • • •

MATERIALS

For each group:

- a pint-size plastic container
- baby food jar with lid
- thermometer
- cold water
- insulating materials (see step 1)

SCIENCE BACKGROUND

Insulators help keep temperatures constant by trapping heat. Again, heat is not the same as temperature. It is the absence or presence of heat that affects temperature and determines whether or not something is hot—or cold. An insulated thermos, then, will keep a hot drink hot by trapping the presence of heat and a cold drink cold by maintaining the absence of heat.

insulator:
a material that helps prevent the loss or transfer of heat; insulators are poor conductors

STEPS

Maybe !!

① A few days before starting this experiment, brainstorm materials that might help keep something cold from warming up. Record students' suggestions on a chart, then invite them to help you collect some of the materials on the list. (You might want to send a note home explaining the activity, listing children's ideas and asking that parents work with children to gather any of the materials they can.) Sand, pebbles, soil, newspaper, cotton, wool socks (or scraps of wool), Styrofoam, and water are just some of the materials students might suggest.

② Divide students into small groups and let each group select a material to test. Make a chart that lists the members of each group and the test material. Leave room to record each group's results.

③ Give each group a pint-size container, thermometer, and baby food jar/lid. Have children follow these directions to test their insulating materials. (For older students, you can copy these directions on chart paper and post.)

- Pour cold water into the baby food jars. Record the temperature of the water, then screw on the lid.

- Place some of the material you are testing in the bottom of the plastic container.

- Put the baby food jar inside the plastic container.

- Stuff the test material all around the baby food jar. Try to fill the space between the plastic container and the baby food jar. (Students who are testing wool socks can wrap the sock around the baby food jar, then place it in the plastic container.)

⊙ Set your container on a sunny windowsill.

④ Have children check the temperature in their jars every 30 minutes for the next two hours and record their data on the chart. (Be sure thermometers have the same starting temperature.)

⑤ Bring children together to discuss results.

⊙ How does the temperature of the water in the jar after two hours compare to the initial temperature of the water?

⊙ If there is a change, what do you think caused it?

⊙ What conclusions can you make about the ability of each material to keep the heat from the sunlight from heating up the cold water? Based on the sample list provided in step 1, water, air, soil, sand, and pebbles are not good insulators. Newspaper, Styrofoam (and other packing materials), and wool are better insulators.

⑥ Follow up by discussing why students think some materials make better insulators. (See Think About It, below.)

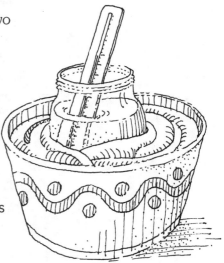

• • • • • • • • •

WINDOW ON CHILD DEVELOPMENT

Primary-age students are typically not ready to differentiate between heat and temperature. (See Activity 1, Science Background, page 49.) What is important for young children to recognize is the usefulness of heat in our lives. Giving students opportunities to connect the idea that light provides heat and heat can make something feel warm will help provide a foundation for later learning about heat as energy.

THINK ABOUT IT

The questions that follow are just some that your students might already be asking. The explanations are intended for your use. You can adapt the information to best meet your students' needs.

Do you think the temperature in a sunny spot will be the same in the afternoon as it is in the morning? Why? The temperatures will probably change as the day progresses and the amount of sunlight changes. In discussing this question, students might be inspired to set up an investigation to test their ideas.

How do you think the temperature on the windowsill compares with the temperature outside? On a sunny day some of the sun's light passes through the classroom windows. Once inside, the light is converted into heat and cannot easily pass back through the window, meaning that the heat builds up in the room, making the windowsill warmer.

What color would you choose to stay warm in winter? Why? Just as light colors will help keep you cooler in summer (by reflecting back sunlight), darker colors will help you feel warmer in cold weather because they absorb sunlight.

Why do you think it gets so hot in the summer? First of all, in the Northern Hemisphere the sun's rays are hitting Earth more directly, resulting in warmer temperatures. This heat is also collected by soil and water, so that by the end of summer they have become saturated and begin to reflect back their stored heat. We call these late summer days the *dog days* of summer. This name comes from the ancient Romans who thought that the late summer temperatures were a result of heat coming from Sirius, the Dog Star, which is summer's brightest star.

EXTENDING THE ACTIVITIES

- Invite students to research how solar energy works and what its applications are. Try building and using solar cookers. (See Resources.)

- Investigate the insulators that help keep heat in (or out of) the school, such as shades, building materials, and so on. Children can follow up with families by conducting a similar investigation at home.

- Explore how the angle of the sun's light affects temperatures and how this is connected with the seasons.

- Learn more about the greenhouse effect, which is related to concepts developed in Activity 1. (Scientists believe that huge quantities of gases in the air are trapping heat and causing changes in the climate.)

RESOURCES

For Children

Exploring Energy by Gallimard Jeunesse (Scholastic, 1993). All kinds of energy are explored in this interactive book, beginning with the sun.

The Sun: Our Nearest Star by Franklyn Branley (HarperCollins, 1988). An easy-to-read book about the importance of the sun in our everyday lives.

For Teachers

Elementary Science Activities for All Seasons by Julia Spencer Moutran (Center for Applied Research in Education, 1990). Includes directions for two different solar cookers.

Supplies

Thermometers
Delta Education, (800) 258-1302
Edmund Scientific, (609) 547-8880

The Sun's Warm Ways

Name_____

DATA COLLECTION SHEET

	Soil	Water	Sand
1. Which cup do you think will collect the most heat?			
2. Which cup do you think will stay coolest ?			
3. Record the initial temperature of each cup.			
4. Record the temperature of each cup after 30 minutes.			
5. Record the final temperature of each cup after one hour.			

Which cup collected the most heat?

Which cup collected the least heat?

How do your results compare with your predictions?

Sowing Seeds

Where do seeds come from? What do seeds need to grow? How are seeds like other living things? The windowsill in your classroom is a natural place for year-round plant investigations. As children plant and tend their windowsill gardens, they'll also develop a sense of responsibility and gain an appreciation for their environment. Students will also discover that there are many different kinds of plants—and that these plants serve a variety of purposes.

PROCESS SKILLS: *observing, classifying, communicating, comparing, measuring, predicting, collecting and recording data, making conclusions*

ACTIVITY 1

From Seed to Plant

In this activity, students plant seeds in clear cups so they can observe what happens when seeds germinate.

MATERIALS

For each team of two:

- clear plastic cups (two cups per student)
- paper towels (one towel per student)
- two or three scarlet runner bean seeds per team (other seeds, such as pea, will work, too)
- several shoe boxes with lids
- string
- strong tape

seed:
the part of a plant that contains a tiny new plant; the new plant, located inside the seed, is called an embryo

germinate:
to start growing; the amount of time it takes a seed to germinate varies from plant to plant

STEPS

① Introduce this activity with a KWL chart. (See Assessing Student Learning, page 60.) Then help children team up with partners (a group of three is fine, too) and gather materials. Each team will need two cups, a paper towel, and a few seeds.

② Demonstrate the following steps as children follow along with their own cups:

- Pour about 1/2 inch of water in the bottom of one cup.

- Fold the paper towel in half two times.

- Wrap the folded paper towel around the outside of the second cup. Slip this cup inside the first cup. The paper towel should touch the water, allowing the paper towel to become moist.

- Place the seeds on the paper towel. Make sure you can see the seeds through the outside cup.

③ Ask students to draw the seed cups in their science journals and record the date.

④ Have students write their initials on their cups (in a spot away from the seeds). Have each team place one seed cup in the box. (Use two boxes if necessary.) Replace the lid and set the box on the windowsill. Ask students to place their other cups directly on the windowsill. Note: Seeds in both places will need to be kept moist. If the paper towels appear at any time to be dried out, students can just pour a little water into the space between the outside and inside cups.

⑤ Ask: What do you think will happen to the seeds in each location? Let students use their journals to record predictions. Let students check on their seed cups daily, writing and/or sketching their observations in their science journals. From what they observe, what do they think seeds need to germinate? Discuss light as a variable in this experiment. Ask: Do seeds needs light to germinate? (No. See Science Background, above.)

⑥ When the bean seeds begin to grow out of the cup, students can remove the inside cup and gently add soil around the seeds in the outside cup. Don't worry about the paper towel. It will begin to break down in the soil and won't be an obstacle for the roots. Let students water their plants and set them back on the windowsill. Attach string so that it runs vertically from the bottom of the windows to the top. (Use strong tape to attach the string to the window.) Place the plants in front of these strings and have children begin to wind the stems around the string. Soon, scarlet runner bean vines will decorate your windowsill center!

SCIENCE BACKGROUND

Students are often surprised to find out that most seeds do not need light to germinate. However, seeds do need moisture (not too much), air, and the right temperature. Under the right conditions germination will occur. The seed will swell, splitting the seed coat and allowing the roots and tiny leaves to emerge. The length of time it takes a seed to germinate varies from plant to plant and depends on proper conditions. Some, like radish and alfalfa, sprout in several days. Others, such as cosmos, may take two or three weeks.

While You're Away
It doesn't take much for seedlings to dry up. Left over a weekend on a windowsill, seedlings will dry up and die. One way to prevent this is to cover the pots loosely with plastic wrap. Or invest in a mini-greenhouse cover (available for a few dollars from gardening supply stores), which is basically a tray for your planters with a plastic domed top.

variable:
a factor in an experiment that can change

⑦ As an extension, invite children and their families to search for seeds in foods at home and then try planting them. (See Windowsill Science at Home, page 65.)

• • • • • • • • • •

Assessing Student Learning Seed investigations like the one described here present a good opportunity for KWL charts. Before doing the activity, use one color of marker to record what the students presently know about seeds. In a second color, record what it is they would like to know more about. At the end of this activity, and throughout the other investigations at this center, use a third color marker to indicate what students learn about seeds.

CURRICULUM CONNECTION: Seeds Add Up (Math)

Have your students figure out how many seeds were planted by the entire class. Depending on the age and ability level of your students, they might simply count (1, 2, 3, . . .) or they can do some multiplication. (We know that each student planted 3 seeds. There are 20 students in our class…) Students can also keep track of how many seeds germinate. Make a picture or bar graph to show how many seeds germinated in each location. Older students can even begin to figure out the percentage of germination for the seeds. This can lead to an investigation of the freshness of seeds as a variable in germination time. (The fresher the seed, the better the germination rate. In fact, most seed packets will have a date stamped on them.)

WINDOW ON CHILD DEVELOPMENT

Elementary students are constantly refining their understandings of what an organism is. Younger students may not, for example, recognize seeds as living things. But as they participate in activities that allow them to examine seeds, plant them, and watch them grow, they will begin to recognize the role a seed plays in the life cycle of a plant. From here, students can begin to understand that one of the identifying characteristics of a living thing is that it grows.

ACTIVITY 2

Greenhouse Growing

Students will discover how warmer temperatures in their own greenhouses speed up germination.

MATERIALS

- three clear plastic cups (for each group)
- mixed birdseed (the kind that contains millet)
- soil
- rulers
- thermometers
- mister bottles
- masking tape

STEPS

① Divide students into groups of two to three for this activity. Ask each group to follow these steps:

- Fill two of the cups with soil.
- Scatter a teaspoon of birdseed over the soil in each of the cups.
- Lightly water both cups using a mister bottle.
- Place a "lid" on one of the cups by placing the third cup upside down on top. Tape the cups together. (Though the cups are taped together, this is not an airtight environment and air will circulate.)

② Ask students to write brief descriptions or draw pictures of this setup in their science journals. In addition, ask them to record their predictions of what they think will happen to the birdseed in both containers.

③ Have each group set the containers on the windowsill. Let students check their cups daily, recording observations in their science journals. Demonstrate how to measure and record the temperature of each cup by inserting a thermometer in the soil for five minutes. Make sure when students measure the temperature in the covered cups that they push the thermometers down far enough so that they can replace the lids and prevent heat from escaping. (After five minutes they can take out the thermometers and again replace the lids.)

④ As birdseed starts to sprout, have students note which seeds germinate first: those in the covered or uncovered cup.

⑤ Over the next week, students can use a ruler to measure the length of the plants in each container. Does the seed in one cup grow more quickly than in the other cup? Why? Share pictures of greenhouses and discuss how they help plants grow. Ask students which of their containers is like a greenhouse.

SCIENCE BACKGROUND

While exploring heat (see The Sun's Warm Ways, page 49), students discovered that as sunlight passes through the classroom window on a sunny day, some of that light is converted into heat. This allows heat to build up in the room. Commercial nurseries and even home gardeners use greenhouses to create this effect—helping to maintain a warm environment for seeds to germinate and plants to grow.

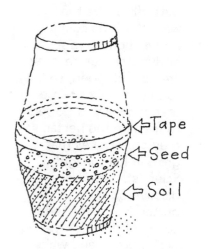

⇦Tape
⇦Seed
⇦Soil

⑥ After several weeks, students can transplant their birdseed plants in a designated place in the school yard or at home.

• • • • • • • • • •

Note: *You can use these mini-greenhouses to introduce the water cycle in action, too. Draw students' attention to how the lids of the covered cups are sometimes clear and at other times are covered with water droplets. Let children try to relate this to their own observations of rain falling, making things wet, and then drying up.*

Assessing Student Learning

Read the "The Garden" from Arnold Lobel's *Frog and Toad Together*. (See Resources.) Have students list Toad's ideas for what he thinks his seeds need in order to grow. Then invite students to discuss what they now think seeds need to grow (moisture, warm temperatures). Based on what they have learned, have them compose a letter to Toad or role-play giving him advice about how he can help his seeds germinate and grow into plants.

ACTIVITY 3

Butterfly Gardens

Now that your students have learned what seeds need to start growing, let them raise plants to create a butterfly garden (plants that attract butterflies). You don't need a large plot of land for this. Students can start the seeds indoors and transplant them into window boxes or pots outside if garden space is not available.

Note: *Because butterflies and flowers both need warm temperatures, you will want to plan this activity so that flowers are blooming in early June. If you live in northern areas, where warmer temperatures may not arrive by the end of the school year, you can plan on having students take their pots home to transplant over the summer. Or plant another type of theme garden. (See suggestions, page 63.) Be sure to get approval ahead of time on an outdoor location for the garden. An area near the school's entrance, a window box hanging from your windowsill, large pots set in sunny locations—all are possibilities.*

• • • • • • • • •

MATERIALS

- *The Butterfly Seeds* (see Resources)
- peat pots, paper cups, or egg cartons (with the cover cut off)
- soil

- seeds (use some of the varieties mentioned in Science Background, page 62)
- newspaper to cover work area

STEPS

① If possible, read *The Butterfly Seeds* by Mary Watson, a lovely story about a grandfather who gives his grandson some butterfly seeds to grow.

② Follow up by asking children if they have ever seen butterflies on a plant. Did they notice anything special about these plants? (Butterflies like plants with flowers.) Share some of the background information about the kinds of plants butterflies prefer.

③ Invite students to start their own butterfly garden on the windowsill. Set out peat pots (or other containers), soil, and "butterfly seeds" for students to plant. (You might want to plan on providing enough materials so that students can plant one pot at school and take one home.) Before students begin planting, review what they know about what seeds and plants need to grow.

④ Have students plant and water the seeds as directed on the package, then set the pots on the windowsill. When plants are well established, have each student transplant a pot outdoors, in the ground, in pots, or in window boxes. Plants in peat pots can be planted directly into the soil. If students are using paper cups, have them peel away the paper from the plants.

• • • • • • • • • •

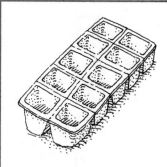

What's a Peat Pot?
Peat pots are handy for germinating seeds. They're small containers sometimes connected to one another, like egg cartons. They're made from peat, different mosses that are used for mulch. When seeds are ready for transplanting, you can put these pots directly in the soil. (They will break down.) Peat pots are inexpensive and are available in gardening-supply stores.

| Assessing Student Learning | Make a photo journal of the butterfly garden project, taking pictures of your young scientists tending |

their gardens. Let children add captions to the photos to show what they have observed. You can focus children's responses and help them reveal what they learned in greater depth and detail by providing prompts for various pictures. You can do this by attaching questions to different photos. For example, next to a photo of a seedling, you can ask: What are two things this seedling needs to grow?

THINK ABOUT IT

The questions that follow are just some that your students might already be asking. The explanations are intended for your use. You can adapt the information to best meet your students' needs.

How do you know if something is a seed? Inside *every* seed,

More Theme Gardens to Grow
Here are some suggestions for additional windowsill theme gardens.

Pizza Garden: *tomatoes, oregano, basil, chives*

Senses Garden: *mint (smell), arugula (taste), marigolds (sight), gourds (sound), lamb's ears (touch)*

ABC's Garden: *A for asters, B for beans, C for cosmos, and so on*

there is a young plant called an embryo. Given the proper conditions, a seed can germinate and grow into a plant.

How do you think seeds are like other living things? Like other living things, seeds need food and water; they grow and develop; and they reproduce themselves.

Where do you think seeds come from? Flowering plants and cone-bearing trees produce seeds. Parts of the flower work together to produce seeds. This includes the fruit which serves to protect the seeds. When the seeds are ready, the fruit ripens and the seeds disperse, continuing the plant's life cycle.

EXTENDING THE ACTIVITIES

- Let students find out how seeds disperse.
- Research plant adaptations.
- Investigate how soil types affect plant growth.

RESOURCES

For Children

The Butterfly Seeds by Mary Watson (Tambourine Books/Morrow, 1995). A grandfather gives his grandson "butterfly seeds" to bring to America. The child plants the seeds in an old crate he turns into a window box and waits for the butterflies to arrive.

Frog and Toad Together by Arnold Lobel (HarperCollins, 1972). There are several wonderful short chapters in this book. One chapter, titled "The Garden," finds Toad worried about his seeds and determined to make them sprout by shouting at them and playing music for the seeds to hear.

Linnea's Windowsill Garden by Christina Bjork (Farrar, Straus & Giroux, 1988). Linnea, a young girl, shares her own seed and plant investigations with readers. Includes many wonderful ideas for young children to try.

For Teachers

Growing Ideas. This newsletter, published by the National Gardening Association, is full of great lesson ideas submitted by classroom teachers. The National Gardening Association also awards grants to classrooms for gardening projects. (800) 538-7476 or e-mail *nga@together.net*

Sunflower Houses by Sharon Lovejoy (Interweave Press, 1991). If you want to do more with gardening in the classroom, this book is full of great ideas, information, and plant lore. Try *Hollyhock Days*, too, by the same author.

Windowsill Science at Home

Dear _____,

At our windowsill science center we are germinating seeds and growing plants to discover what seeds and plants need to grow. You can enrich your child's understanding about seeds with this fun and easy activity. (And you can do it while you're enjoying your breakfast or dinner!) Here's what to do:

1. As you and your child are preparing or eating a meal, try to spot seeds in some of the foods, such as raw peanuts, beans, squash, cucumbers, watermelon, or sugar snap peas.

2. When you find seeds, place them on a paper towel to let them dry. Write each seed's name next to it.

3. Select some seeds to plant together. Just follow these steps:

- You'll need a paper cup (egg cartons work well, too) and some soil to germinate the seeds.

- Plant each seed about 1/4 inch under the soil (one or two per cup or egg carton cup). Moisten the soil and place the container(s) in a sunny, warm spot (but not next to or on a heater).

- Invite your child to draw a picture of what the seeds might look like when they sprout. How many days does your child think it will take?

Thanks for working on this science activity with your child.

Sincerely,

Windowsill Picnic

This collection of activities celebrates students' ongoing windowsill science discoveries. From discovering how the sun provides light and warmth to recognizing what seeds need to grow, students will apply what they've learned in preparing a picnic to share. They'll make evaporation connections as they use the sun's heat to dry apples. They'll also use the sun to steep tea and make bread dough (and discover that tiny organisms—like yeast—don't just live in ponds). They'll germinate edible sprouts to enjoy, as well.

PROCESS SKILLS: *observing, communicating, comparing, predicting, measuring, collecting and recording data, making conclusions*

Sprouts to Eat

About one week before the picnic, let students apply their seed-germinating skills to grow some edible sprouts.

MATERIALS

- reclosable sandwich bags (one bag per group)
- sprouting seeds (alfalfa, radish, mung, and mustard are all possibilities)
- hole-punch
- permanent marker

- large bowl of water (or sinkful)
- string (one 10-inch piece of string for each group)

Note: *Just before the activity, fill a bowl with warm water and set it on the windowsill.*

STEPS

① Have students work in small groups to prepare sprouts. Guide them in completing the following steps:

- Cut three small triangles out of the bottom of the sandwich bag. This will provide drainage for the water.
- Use the hole-punch to make a hole just under the seal of the bag.
- Write group members' initials on the bag with the marker.
- Add about 1/4 cup of seeds to your bag.
- Seal the bag and place it in the bowl of warm water. Leave the bags in the bowl overnight.

② The next morning, have a student from each group hold the bag over the bowl until all of the water has drained out of the bag. Help students run string through the holes in their bags and hang them on the clothesline. (See pages 38–39.) Place the bags in a dark place, such as a closet, for a couple of days. Explain that this is where the seeds will germinate.

③ Ask students how many days they think it will take for the seeds to germinate. Record their guesses.

④ Have students check seeds daily and record observations. They can rinse the seeds with water once or twice a day to keep them moist.

⑤ Once the beans have sprouted (probably three to five days), hang the bags in the windowsill center (from the clothesline). After several days the sprouts will be green and ready to eat.

Have students write or draw directions for sprouting seeds to eat. Attach their cards to small bags of seeds they can take home.

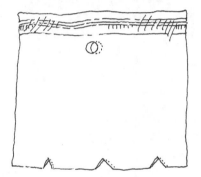

SCIENCE BACKGROUND

Plants are an important part of our diets. When we eat plants, we may be eating different fruits, flowers, roots, leaves, or seeds. Tomatoes and apples are fruits. Artichokes and broccoli are flowers. Carrots and beets are roots. Spinach and arugula are leaves. Peas and beans are seeds. In this activity, students will be planting seeds that germinate quickly—with sprouts ready for eating in just a few days.

CURRICULUM CONNECTION:
Classifying Foods (Math/Language Arts)

Share Science Background (above) with students. Then brainstorm fruits and vegetables they eat, recording students' contributions on a chart. Let students cut out pictures of some of these foods from magazines. For younger students, place the pictures on a tray at the center and invite them to work with partners to classify the foods. Can they find foods that are flowers? Roots? Leaves? Fruits? Seeds? You might make sorting mats for each category, including a sample picture of each. Older students can use journals to keep track of the flowers, roots, leaves, fruits, and seeds in their diets.

Drying Apples (Social Studies/Math)

For hundreds of years, people have preserved food by drying it. Drying food eliminates moisture that can cause mold to grow and food to spoil. Let students discover how evaporation helps dry and preserve food by mking dried apple rings. Simple directions follow.

- About a week before your picnic, peel some apples and slice into rings. Ask children to predict how much the apples weigh now and how much they will weigh after they dry. Weigh the apples. Record the weight.

- Have children work together to string the apple rings. Use clothespins to attach the string of apple rings to the clothesline at your windowsill center. (See page 39.) Make sure the slices don't touch one another.

- Drape cheesecloth over the apples to keep dust and flies off the fruit.

- Observe what happens to the apples. (They'll shrink in size and wrinkle as water evaporates.) Talk about where the water goes. (It turns into water vapor.)

- After the apples are dried, weigh them. What do students think causes the change in weight? (Loss of water.) Enjoy the apples at your picnic!

ACTIVITY 2

Rising Bread Dough

While making bread for the windowsill picnic, students will learn how yeast, a single-celled organism, and warm air help dough rise. You can make the dough the day before or start it the morning of the picnic.

> **fungus:**
> a single-celled organism that does not make its own food, like green plants do

MATERIALS

- ingredients for bread dough (see Bread Recipe)
- one package of active dry yeast (in addition to two packages for the bread)
- two baby food jars

- measuring cups and spoons
- two large bowls
- waxed paper (to cover table/work area)
- cooking oil
- two wooden spoons
- ruler

Bread Recipe

2 packages active dry yeast
(check date to make sure
it is fresh)

4 cups warm water

pinch of sugar

4 teaspoons salt

10 to 12 cups flour

Note: *Before the activity, consider making task cards for the students. This will make it easier for everybody to participate. You will probably want to set up two workstations and divide students into two groups, one at each station. (In this case, make two sets of task cards.) Invite a couple of parents or older students to help manage the stations.*

STEPS

1. How many students have/had bread in their lunches today? Talk about different kinds of breads students like. (This is a good time for a survey on favorite breads or sandwiches, crust/no crust, and so on. Compile, graph, and display results.)

2. Before making the bread, demonstrate what happens to yeast when you add sugar. First, fill the two baby food jars with warm water. Label one jar "sugar" and the other "no sugar." Add 1/2 package of yeast to each jar. Add a pinch of sugar to the jar labeled "sugar." Have students observe and describe what happens in both jars. (The yeast in the jar with sugar will foam up. Students will be able to smell the yeast.) Explain that yeast plays an important role in making some kinds of bread. The reaction that they are observing is what helps bread dough to rise.

3. Have children follow these steps to mix the bread dough. (You can write these directions on task cards.)

   - Measure 1/4 cup of warm water and pour it into each of the bowls.

   - Dissolve 2 teaspoons of sugar in each of the bowls.

   - Add a package of yeast to both of the bowls. Stir to mix in the yeast, then let it sit for a couple of minutes. (Take a break for observations now. Ask students to describe what is happening. Within a minute you should start to see the

SCIENCE BACKGROUND

Yeast is classified as a fungus, a single-celled living organism. It cannot manufacture its own food like green plants can. In order for the yeast to grow, it has to be fed. This is why sugar is sometimes added to recipes that contain yeast. As yeast feeds on sugar, alcohol and carbon dioxide are formed. This reaction is called *fermentation*, and it is what lets bread dough rise. Yeast likes a warm environment between 100°F and 110°F. When making bread, this is best achieved by placing the dough in a warm place (like on a sunny windowsill) and covering it with a cloth.

yeast multiplying and bursting to the surface of the water.)

- Add 2 3/4 cups water to each bowl.

- Mix in 5 to 6 cups flour and 2 teaspoons salt in each bowl. (Add the flour a little at a time. The dough should be a little sticky.)

- Stir until the flour is mixed in well, then turn out onto the waxed paper.

- Coat hands with oil and knead the dough for 10 to 15 minutes. Add a little more flour if the dough is too sticky to handle. (Students will have fun taking turns with this.)

- Return the dough to clean, oiled bowls, use tape to mark the dough height on the outside of the bowls, and cover each with a cloth. Set one in a sunny windowsill. Set the second somewhere cool. (If your room is fairly warm, you may wish to put the second bowl of dough in a refrigerator.) Ask students to predict what they think will happen to the dough in both bowls. Let the dough sit for about 1 1/2 hours.

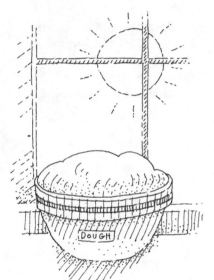

④ After 1 1/2 hours, check both bowls of dough. Let students make observations and describe the dough. How does the original height of each compare with the height now? Why do students think the dough in the sunny window grew but the other one stayed just about the same? (Warmer temperatures increase yeast productivity.)

⑤ Divide the dough that has risen in half. Let students shape these halves into loaves. Place loaves on an oiled baking sheet (or one sprinkled with cornmeal), cover with a cloth, and set on the windowsill. Let rise again until doubled (about another hour).

⑥ Bake the loaves at 350°F for about 45 minutes. The bread will sound hollow when tapped on if it is done.

• • • • • • • • • •

Assessing Student Learning | Help students apply what they've learned about yeast as well as review the sequence and process of bread making by finding a way to make the second bowl of bread dough rise. As students discuss options, ask them to review their observations of both bowls. What can they change to make the second bowl of dough rise? (Place it in a warm spot.) After the dough rises, students can use it to shape their own mini-loaves to bake. While the bread bakes, invite children to write stories about their day baking bread. Encourage them to include details from their experience.

Tea and Sunshine

The day of the picnic, your students can explore infusion by making sun tea to drink. The sun helps out by providing the warmth needed to make the flavor from the tea bags mix with water.

infusion:
a substance that is dissolved in water

● ● ● ● ● ● ● ● ●

MATERIALS

- ◉ two clear gallon containers
- ◉ 20 herbal tea bags
- ◉ water
- ◉ lemon and sugar (optional)

STEPS

① Fill both containers with water. Add ten tea bags to each container. Ask students to observe the container and draw what they see in their journals.

② Set one container on a sunny windowsill and one in a dark, cool place. Ask students to predict what will happen in each container.

③ Let students check the containers after a half hour. What do they notice? Again, have children record observations in their journals. (The water in the windowsill container will be infused with the color of the tea more quickly than the water in the dark. If students touch the containers, they will find that the container on the windowsill is warmer.)

④ Have children check again after a couple of hours and record observations. How do the two containers compare with each other? (Students will see that the tea in the windowsill jar is more blended than the tea in the dark.) How do students' observations of each container compare with those made two hours ago? Ask students to explain what they think is happening.

⑤ Take the container that was in the dark, cool place and set it on the windowsill to speed up the infusion process. Students can serve both containers of tea at their picnic!

● ● ● ● ● ● ● ● ●

WINDOW ON CHILD DEVELOPMENT

The activities in this center invite children to revisit many of the concepts introduced in earlier centers, including those related to light and heat (*see* The Way Light Works, page 43, and The Sun's Warm Ways, page 49), evaporation and the water cycle (*see* Evaporation Investigations, page 35), seeds (*see* Sowing Seeds, page

SCIENCE BACKGROUND

Tea is an example of an infusion, the dissolving of a substance in water. When placed in water, the tea leaves begin to break apart, releasing flavor and color into the water. The warmer the water, the more quickly the flavor and color blend through the water. This is because the warmer the water, the faster the water molecules move. This motion moves the dissolved tea through the water helping to create an even mixture.

58), and microscopic life (see Tiny Worlds, page 26). Revisiting concepts throughout the year gives children a chance to clear up misconceptions and allows them to build on their experiences to strengthen understandings.

THINK ABOUT IT

The questions that follow are just some that your students might already be asking. The explanations are intended for your use. You can adapt the information to best meet your students' needs.

Can you think of reasons people dry food? Dehydrated (or dried-out) food is used by astronauts and hikers. Why? It is easy to pack, it's lightweight, and it doesn't spoil. Children who snack on raisins or fruit leather are also enjoying dried food.

Where do you think yeast comes from? Yeast is often found growing on fruits, where it can feed on the fruits' natural sugars. There are many different strains of yeast.

What are some ways the sun helps us? The sun provides us with light, which helps us see things. Sunlight is also essential for plants to grow and to warm our planet. In fact, the sun allows life to exist on our planet.

EXTENDING THE ACTIVITIES

- Find out what kinds of foods astronauts take into space. Sample some!
- Investigate the wide variety of breads that make up the diets of different peoples around the world.
- Investigate the health benefits of different kinds of foods. Children can create sample healthy-meal menus. Plan and prepare one of the meals. Invite parents to be your guests.

RESOURCES

A *Turkey for Thanksgiving* by Eve Bunting (Houghton Mifflin, 1991). This would be a fun book to share at your picnic. It is about another celebration, Thanksgiving, that is hosted by Mr. and Mrs. Moose. What is served for dinner will be a surprise for the reader who is expecting turkey.

What Food Is This? by Rosemarie Hausherr (Scholastic, 1994). This book will inspire children to think about foods and where they come from. Rich color photographs of children from many cultures add to the book's appeal.